CW00494514

The Coming of the Feminine Christ

The Coming

of the

Feminine Christ

by

niamh clune

amrita publications inc.

Published in 1998 by Amrita Publications Inc.
Beach Ave; Vancouver, British Columbia, Canada.
e-mail: amrita@ethericweb.com
            clune@amrita.co.uk

Distributed internationally on the World Wide Web:
www.ethericweb.com

Cover design by Stef Michalski
e-mail: stef@room237.demon.co.uk

Copy design by Niamh Clune
Technical Advisor, Doug Johnson

Canadian Cataloguing in Publication Data:

Clune, Niamh, 1952-
    The coming of the feminine Christ

ISBN 0-9684420-0-5

    1. Feminist spirituality. 2. Transpersonal psychology. 3. Mysticism.
I. Title.
BF204.7.C58 1998   150.19'8   C98-911084-2

Printed and bound in Canada by New West Press.

Amrita Publications Inc. is a newly founded company, dedicated to publishing the works of Amrita as authored by Niamh Clune.

For

Aleisha and Doug

With special thanks to the following:

Karen Twining, Phil and Liz McFie, Mary Davies, Karen Isles, Francis Aloisio, Natasha Gellatly, Ardith Beynon, Catherine Morris, Dianne Brooke-Webster. And last, but not least, *Mary Gregory.*

The Coming of the Feminine Christ

Table of Contents

Book Three

Voyage of a Seer

Book Four

Symbols of Transformation

Book Five

Revelation

Introduction

All souls are tongues of Christ's great flame,
sparks of Christ's great life,
seeking expression in the world of shadows.

The soul made flesh
incarnating through each of us
is the Word made flesh,
the gift of thought and speech.
Thus is wo-man exalted,
made God,
yearning to give expression
to her and his soul.

amrita

In order to do justice to the profound vision that inspired this work, I have made a humble attempt at magic. To make words appear on an empty page required them to be plucked—often unwillingly, from the ethers, and cajoled into clothing images emblazoned by the light of my soul upon my inner eye.

Words are particularly difficult little creatures to organise. They have minds and wills of their own and will misbehave if not given proper respect. Some of them have inferiority complexes! Usually, it is the large words that engage the writer's efforts. Then the little words feel ignored. Out of spite they will change the sense of something so subtly. This is why, out of politeness, I have tried to court them by avoiding the larger and more impressive words that strut across the page creating the illusion of self-importance.

Thus in order to alleviate their usually boring task, I called on the little words, and engaged them in creative activity. I invited them to paint pictures of demons and souls. Hopefully, I have solicited them to serve my cause.

Sometimes, I was forced to discipline them, for I needed to orchestrate them in such a way as to convey mighty themes—dark as well as light. When they received respectful, yet firm attention, they performed beautiful symphonic melodies with underlying haunting, repetitive themes.

I have packed profound ideas into simple, pithy sentences. If at first, reader, you do not grasp them, be patient. This is a book to read again and again.

The Word was made Flesh means that Christ—the Soul—was incarnated into animal form. Thus humankind was granted the potential to be raised in consciousness beyond the beast; for we had received the divine gift of speech. The ancient Greeks knew the Word as *logos,* which is the expression of the Mind of God. The Word is thus the embodiment of divine revelation—the incarnation of Christ consciousness.

The Coming of the Feminine Christ is written in the old way, in the way of druidic tradition, when words were considered magical, musical and mystical. The ancient tellers of esoteric wisdom understood the importance of the philosophical root meanings of the Word. They passed those meanings down the ages with great care in story telling rituals in order to preserve the inborn knowledge hidden in the collective soul.

Words have power. When written or spoken in a way that respects this truth, they will convey meaning on many levels of consciousness at once. In this book, the Word is used as a catalyst and image-maker to paint pictures of not only the radiant soul and the way of transformation, but uncompromisingly, the darker, treacherous reality of the unconscious.

Prepare your imagination, therefore, to travel inner worlds. Therein, grant its sighting of ancient esoteric mysteries. Allow it to participate in deep soul-making dramas. For these are the makings of our futures.

niamh clune

2

Book one

Prophesies & Visions

One

The Angel in the Forest

West Coast of Vancouver Island...

We entered the virgin rain forest.

No human interference had ever had effect on that green and alien world so full of its own power. It was a living monument to nature.

Huge gnarled roots had clawed a giant ridge out of the earth. The ground plunged sharply away on either side.

We climbed the maze of roots and crunched fallen leaves into the hardening autumn earth. We followed the forest ridge as it dipped to the ocean—to rocks and sea lion caves. Pacific waves crashed the shore. And we watched. And all of nature's progeny basked in lukewarm sun.

From the moment we had entered the forest, I felt a sense of unease that stayed with me all of that long day.

Dusk fell. It was time to return. We made our way back along the ridge.

Up ahead, a shimmering lit the trees. We moved towards it.

An angel of brilliant yellow light appeared. I knelt, overawed by its terrible power. Bound by its luminosity, I was compelled to participate. I felt my mind open. I felt alien thoughts enter inside my head.

The angel transferred its thoughts in Colours, emblazoning them on the innermost reaches of my soul:

> *I am an archangel*
> *of the life-chain that has for millions of years*

5

been guardians of nature, custodians of the world.
We have nurtured mass life:
trees, dolphins, sea lions.
We have presided over the development of the human body.

Our tasks are complete.
We have achieved liberation.
We are leaving the earth forever.

Already, I am light years away.
My power burns from worlds beyond.
You feel only an echo of my former presence.

My perfection is death
to all that is considered
to be human.

A shard of the angel's yellow light pierced our hearts. Its message, delivered from the universe, froze us to the core:

I am the last angel of my kind.
Humankind is desolate.
By your wills, the planet lives or dies.
Only the awakened heart will avert the apocalypse.

It passed me a cylindrical object of light—and the duty to relay the weight, enormity and depth of its message to others.

Two

A Meeting with Destiny

Wracking, sobbing, tearing doubts of my own sanity
eat into my soul.
Why me?
I cry from the deep, so that only the night shall hear.
Leave me alone!
I am an ordinary person.

Angels don't visit ordinary people.

I fight to hang on to the thin sliver of me that remains,
lest I be forever extinguished by God.

So beautiful, yet so terrible.
What do I do with such a vision?
I am demolished.
Whoever I was is no more.
How can I express the might of it?
What form can I give it to make it expressible to others?
Yet I must.
I must clothe it that it may come into the world,
shaped out of the heavens,
out of an ocean of light,
out of formlessness,
millions of light years away.

Alien, how can I understand?
My mind is turned around.
I have nothing of my own reality to hang on to.
Nothing more to grasp.
And I cannot even grasp you.
I can only submit.
For you are almighty.

God! I never knew.
How can mortals know you?
I regret I ever wanted to.
Am I to be destroyed for looking upon your face?
I would die seeing as I see now:
an ocean of light.
And your thought is at the centre.
Just one thought that carries such profound weight
that I am blown away as a speck of dust,
shrivelled, humbled, terrified.

Go away God!
How dare you rape me in this way?
Demanding that I,
a mere mortal,
should look upon you and try to understand...

My partner had accompanied me into the forest.

Years after this event, the struggle to understand what had happened that day would sear our hearts and minds with unanswerable questions. I could not speak of the angel to anyone. I was miserably haunted by my own inability to convey its message. The beautiful visioned object passed to me by the angel was symbolic of the passing of its knowledge to the human chain. Yet as years passed, it came to symbolise the immense burden of responsibility that would come to weigh so unbearably heavy on my very ordinary shoulders. I felt imposed on—raped by an outside, alien force that had violated all I once believed in. Who would want to listen to such an experience? Who would believe it? How could I expect others to understand, when I could not? I was surrounded by contradictions.

All too often, New Age books described hosts of angels entering into healing rooms. I wondered what these books were really referring to, when our experience of just one angel had been so apocalyptic. We felt alone—let down by superficial testimonials, which were in such poignant contrast to our own experience.

I was looking for answers so that I would no longer feel singled out. None of the New Age material I read on the subject of angels embraced the appalling reality of being communicated with by such a Being. This angel was omnipotent. To personify it in clumsy or even lightweight terms would diminish its power and reality. Therefore, it was to the poets and prophets of Biblical weight that I turned, in order to gain reference to the reality of this Being from the universe who radiated so awesome a life-force. The angel could have destroyed us. None could be in the presence of such a Being without risking personal desolation, mental and physical. Angels are of a life-chain so alien to our own. The vibration of this Being was so refined in comparison to the density of our own pitch, that it felt as if a million volts had fleetingly touched my tiny twelve-volt system. Its perfection was devastating to the natural chaos of human emotions.

A meeting with destiny is often strange and haphazard. It is something over which the conscious mind has no control.

It was already late autumn on Vancouver Island. That particular day, a friend had called to take us into the forest. I was reluctant to go. However, reflecting on the experience later, we realised the event had been inevitable. Our meeting meant the angel's liberation. That longtime prisoner of earth would not be released from its bondage until it had delivered its message. Only then could it hand over responsibility for the future of the planet.

The angel needed Initiates of the ancient wisdom who would understand the angelic language of *Colour.*

For years I had been a practitioner of healing. I had undergone spiritual initiation into the sacred mysteries. Nothing, however, could have prepared me for this event. Years would pass. I would ache with struggle. I could not accept that I had been chosen to be the angel's emissary.

New ageism had already appropriated the idea of angels. I did not know, therefore, how I would bring the message to others. The power and potency of such an event as this ever occurring had already been watered down—split off from its historical, spiritual context.

The angel had delivered an unpopular—terrifying message. *The angels have abandoned us, leaving us desolate.* This truth would counter popular

9

beliefs, emotional needs and unquestioned assumptions. Even the most rational amongst us *want* to believe in angels. We *need* somebody to be out there.

Our need for angels reflects our already sensed, underlying spiritual despair. Somewhere in our collective unconsciousness, we *know* we are abandoned. But we deny it. We have twisted the message—made it into new age fantasy that denies the dark side of where we are in our planetary evolution.

We have thus created an economic boom in angels. Angels are everywhere—as are aliens, space ships and all manner of extraterrestrial illusion. Are we unconsciously trying to compensate for our loss?

The angel's message robs us all of the idea of invisible masters, saviours, or celestial beings waiting to come to the rescue. The angel was cold. The message was hard—forcing us to face reality—*by our wills, the planet lives or dies.*

For days after the experience, my partner and I could not get physically warm. We sat huddled over a wood stove, frozen with shock and fear for the future of the earth. The angel's message had forced us to recognise that humankind is spiritually immature—too immature to husband nature's resources wisely.

Divinity sleeps in us…

My partner and I left Canada and returned to England. From there we went to work in Africa. The situation in South Sudan had worsened—another drought, another famine—and still the war raged with the North. Previously, my partner had worked in South Sudan for Oxfam. Again he would take up an Oxfam post, this time as Country Representative for South Sudan.

From the protected life we had led in Canada, living on five acres of forested land, we plunged into the middle of African reality. We had no psychological protection against what we saw or experienced there. Both of us carried the aching burden of the angel's message in our hearts. We were witnessing what humankind was capable of. Our experience in Africa only reinforced our desolation. We saw corruption, violence, poverty, starvation and death. It soaked into our skins.

We were always aware of the suffering around us. And there was no psychic refuge in which to shelter.

Amidst all that, however, we also met individuals who were exceptional human beings. These individuals were able to continue loving others amidst the madness of war, disease and famine. Somehow, in this context, their humanity stood out in relief against the backdrop of despair. In them we witnessed the human spirit stand triumphant against all the odds. Alas, those truly human, brave spirits were all too few.

During those six years in Africa, we were rootless—belonging nowhere. We struggled to cope with the destruction of African cultures, yet were unable to relate to our own. We were world servers living a paradox— without hope for the future of humankind, yet immersed in its suffering. Humankind was as yet too unconscious to assume the mantle of responsibility for the future. The angels were gone. Our protection was gone. My partner and I carried this secret in the depths of our hearts. We could never do enough. The situation in Africa was a huge dark chasm that swallowed hope, love and creative enterprise.

Again, we returned to England.

Nine years have passed since the angel's appearance. We have heard since that the forest in which the angel appeared has been logged.

For all these years, I have struggled to find a way to convey the angel's impelling message in all its depth and meaning. I have despaired that it would be trivialised. Now, I must release it to the world, and hope that it is received in the spirit in which it is offered.

Many strands of esoteric mystery weave the background to this prophecy. In the attempt to impart the full enormity of this prophetic experience, I have stitched my personal story into this tapestry of events—only that it may serve as a metaphor. Thus the story takes us back in time to the psychological beginnings that had left me fragmented, wounded and hungry enough to fire a spiritual calling.

Three
Early Awakenings

Dublin 1955...

Banging and shouting coming from downstairs woke me. I had heard the noise before. Something was wrong. Filled with an eerie calm of sudden knowing, a voice inside me said, "Now it begins." These were words of an old part of my self—perhaps an ancient knowing that this was destiny working itself out.

I was three years old and deeply sad. I had been wrenched from the arms of unconsciousness that had cradled me for so few baby years, to the realisation that the man who was screaming downstairs was my father—savagely beating my mother.

I crept downstairs and looked through the banisters. The kitchen door was open. My mother was hunched in the corner. Her arms were over her head in an attempt at self-protection. My father jettisoned the kitchen table across the room. It caught my mother and levelled her to the floor. My father ran over to her. His fists came raining down on her. I heard their brutal thud. Vicariously, I felt the relentless violent intent in them crush her flesh and bone.

I ran into the bright lights of the kitchen. I was never a child again...

Throughout my childhood, into my young woman years, my father's obscene violence continued. Shaped by the suffering of my mother, I would become a healer. Compulsively, I would attempt to rescue my mother through the lives of other battered, bruised and broken women who could not defend themselves.

13

I had split off from my own pain—relegated it to unconsciousness. Eventually, I learned that emotional pain needs to be fully encountered, its underlying causes purged with tears. When entered into with understanding, pain's nature is transformed.

Revisiting that earliest memory in later years taught me the paradoxical nature of being the healer and sacred psychologist. In the struggle to love and heal others, I would need to learn to heal myself. Knowledge of self—of one's own personal issues—their dark side and light—brings with it sacred knowledge. It brings insight into the *Greater Self*.

The healing work I later did reflected a new approach. Instead of the focus being upon myself as the powerful healer able to take away other people's pain, I developed a new healing method that engaged clients as active participants in their own healing process. I led them into their own experience of the pain that was locked in muscles, tissues and vital organs.

Earliest memories are essential clues to full psychophysical healing. In these memories is the *matrix* of all we will live out in the future. Earliest memories, however, are easily denied, locked in the body, committed to unconsciousness.

If those around us mishandle our childhood emotional life, we are forced to psychically split off from the pain of those events. Emotional pain is, however, forever held in the body, in endocrine reaction. Every cell, muscle and organ remembers.

This splitting off is popularly called *denial*.

Four

The Story of Denial

As young heroes setting out into life, we relate to the outside world through our sense perceptions. These are the five senses of *touch, taste, sight, sound and smell.* And these are the tools of learning about and defining our physical environment.

But we also have a sixth sense. This is a *psychic sense.* It is an organ of subtle perception. Through it we *feel* the unseen. We pass through an open window and glimpse the inner world, and vision for a moment the *strangeness* of that other reality.

The psychic sense knows no boundaries and has no perspective. It is a nebulous thing, and lives its life unvalued by the physical world. However, a child senses the things lurking beyond the horizon of her/his safe world. Dreams are filled with creatures from that *other place.* The child cannot define what s/he perceives. As yet, the feeling function in the child is undeveloped and immature.

Yet this subtle sense is extremely *sensitive,* relating only to those unshaped, unknowable things that lurk beneath the world under-mind. This is a timeless world that coexists with our world of waking reality. It is the world of undefined emotional chaos—a world in which painful memories slink unloved and unwanted. They know we don't want to see or feel them. We have forever banished them to that *other world* where they remain, elusively weaving their way in and out of enormous trees that block out the sun—weaving patterns of pain and disease.

This world is filled with undefined psychic smells of things rotten and evil. For our negative thoughts live there too. And dreams, desires and aspirations fight it out on an *astral* battleground of hope and despair.

This is our heaven, hell and purgatory. Good girls and boys dream of going there when they die, to the *heaven* they have created for themselves. Bad girls and boys are condemned—by their own guilt—to *purgatory* or to *hell.*

This home is peopled with spectres of the past that live on in *astral bodies*. Some are blinded and alone, eternally suffering the pain of self-created emotional fantasies. Guilt waits to attack them around every curve. Fury rends them apart. Lust teases and taunts with every fantasy ever created by them. They live there too, the fantasies—the contorted apparitions. All they do for eternity is play out the acts that were choreographed for them by the minds of their ingenious makers. Whilst greed, envy and hatred are the vicious voyeurs. They entertain their wandering creators along their lonely paths of pointlessness. And they can conjure up anything.

Hell, Heaven and Purgatory are our thought creations. They are states of being. They exist only in the collective unconscious. This inner world is a reflection both of the soul and of the denied demon shadow of Humanity. In it, things are not measured against physical reality, for this world has nothing to compare itself with.

All of us tacitly receive intrusive emotional images from each other. We do this with the psychic sense. It is our *feeling connection* with the unconscious inner world. It is the organ through which we perceive the atmospheres that move between subjective and objective realities. As we pass into adulthood, we often split off from the imaginal world in order to enter into physical, rational reality. The sixth sense is neglected—often despised. It remains undeveloped and cannot thus be trusted to be our guide through the undergrowth of the unconscious.

Atmosphere is our childhood seedbed. It grows brilliance and imagination. As children, we live predominantly in the *astral world* of intangible emotional atmospheres in which the demons lurk always ready to take possession of us when we are not looking. Our eyes grow big as moons. Somehow, we are protected if our eyes shine into the dark like bright moons. Maybe they can penetrate the gloom of gathering shadows. Ghosts hide in the wardrobe and come out as soon as the light is out, dark and menacing, in the far corner. But we are too afraid to get out of bed and run to comforting arms. For if we do, our ankle will be grabbed by terror—the cold demon who waits under the bed.

With no boundaries or sense of perspective, the sixth sense works like a psychic sponge absorbing everything around it. It will reach upstairs into the attic to touch every buried thought and memory that floats there. No packing case, or hidden chest, or discarded garment of the dead is too much effort to feel out. The deft fingers of the psychic sense reach into everything. And downstairs into the cellar—where people hoard—and the demons of greed must be discovered and experienced by the fear in the child.

Children demonstrate their lack of psychic perspective in their drawings. Tiny trees and huge houses, big fat Ma's with small heads, tall skinny Da's with large heads express the inner landscape of the child. The reason for this is not only because the child can't yet draw, but also because the child is truly expressing the way s/he perceives reality. The mammy may have a large body and a small head because the child relates very much to the body of mother. The daddy has a large head and a skinny body because the body of father does not play much of a part in the child's physical, personal nourishment. The house looms large in the psyche of the child because it is more important than a tree. It is home and shelter.

Because of this lack of psychic perspective, the unnamed fear or hurt in the psyche of the parents becomes a giant bogeyman of fear in the child's unconscious. Not only does the child have to deal with its own hurts, but with those that have been denied and repressed and passed on from the parental unconscious. Unresolved tension, blocked feelings and repressed anger lurk about the house and threaten the child's psychic sense of security. Resentments, frustrations, unrecognised guilt, insecurity and undealt-with hurts are the parents' denials that make their impact upon the child's sensitive feeling body. And they are magnified out of all proportion within the psyche of a little person living in a very big world with no protection from the demons that come in the night. A child cannot define "I'm scared." All s/he knows is an all-pervading emotional sense of fear and threat.

Emotional reverberations ripple throughout the child's watery inner feeling world like the circles of cause and effect created by stones thrown into a lake, or puddles that are jumped on to make them splash. They are stab wounds in the dark—psychic attacks from unseen monsters passed on to the child from the parent's unconscious, as they had been passed to the parents by their ancestors.

These are habitual patterns of thought—the *emotional and psychological DNA* of the psyche—whose phenomenon has been referred to throughout the ages in various wisdom teachings as *Karma*.

17

As children, these patterns mold our lives. They are powerful relic contents of the psyche passed on through atmospheres that remain totally out of perspective because of the immaturity and disrespect of the sixth sense. And no rationalisation in the world can remove childhood fears. They live on as looming shadows, unspoken, unnamed, unconscious.

Every family has its dysfunctional psychology. Few of us are as yet masters of our unconscious. Even if we were born into the smoothest of families, unresolved ancestral pain is the psychic inheritance of us all.

Obviously, some families are more dysfunctional than others. However even a calm and reasonable family can have a devastating but unseen effect on the psyche of the child. In this case, the child growing into adulthood cannot name its psychic discomfort. S/he cannot identify the psychic imposition of invisible family expectations.

Children are powerless to defend themselves against the *dead weight of the unspoken word.* Tacit expectations are hidden enemies that take on monstrous proportions. The growing child cannot confront them. They hang stagnant in the air—silent and suffocating. The unformed identity of the child is often violated by this kind of psychic control. This may not be physical abuse, but it is psychic abuse.

Psychic wounds are more difficult to identify than physical ones and are often harder to heal. A child's headaches, hay fever, asthma, backaches are *negative coping mechanisms* that will cast their shadow over adult life.

Negative coping mechanisms often manifest as somatic symptoms. These symptoms are the keys to our denials. We develop the somatic symptoms, which may manifest as real tissue damage or disease, rather than face the spiritual, bloodline, psychological issue that underlies the manifestation of the disease. Rather, we have been taught by our parents to simply deny emotional pain for fear of upsetting the status quo.

The unspoken pain that surrounds us in childhood is so great that we shut the door on it. And there it stays, locked in dark inner rooms, glowering and dampened and turning in on itself. We lock it in—in order to shut it out. This we must do for protection. But in effect, a child's subtle feeling body is frozen in the painful experience, trapped in a state of inner shock.

Denial happens naturally, in a moment of overwhelming emotional pain, when fate stamps its claim upon its victim. And the potential we might have realised is crushed beneath the weight of fate's dark and heavy hand. There is a moment of conscious recognition. The soul has entered the body for the first time. In a fleeting moment the child knows what the world wills for it. The child has momentarily awakened to suffering.

Most people, however, do not remember this moment. But in this moment is found the key to our psyche and to our fate. This is the moment when fate overwhelmed the little budding self.

Fate, the impostor, rapes the psyche. The bargain is sealed—our fate agreed to—in the moment of denial, in the moment of emotional reaction to intervening circumstances. Fate makes us its victim. It plays us out, forcing us to repeat the past again and again. Whilst destiny is our future. In the seeds of destiny is the undiluted potential of all we might be. But these seeds are buried beneath the weight of that earliest experience. There they lie, dormant, waiting to be touched by a consciousness that has dissolved fate's imposition.

Pain we have all experienced as children, either subtly, or physically, is too great, too overpowering, and there is no way we can deal with it other than denial. Thus, ancestral complexes are recreated in the child's unconscious. These are the young Hero's inherited patterns and tendencies that will have to be lived out. Thus the negative psychic patterns of our ancestors will be repeated by future generations.

The science of *right relationship* is a *new* spiritual psychology. It is a process of becoming who we were always meant to be. The process begins when we awaken to our pain. In our earliest beginnings is the matrix of all we will be. If we deny those atmospheres surrounding our beginnings, we remain victims of our fate rather than becoming the masters of our destiny.

Meeting our denials is a deep *soul-making* drama. It is the initiation into adulthood. It requires us to meet again those fleeting moments, when in childhood the soul first spoke its quiet internal message. It is our task to heal those denials, lest they become the negative psychic inheritance of our children.

19

Five

A Life Repeated

Denial is inner abuse. Synchronistically, it attracts abusers from the outside world.

They feel familiar.

They are outward reflections of our own *sub-personalities*—fragmented parts of the psyche that constitute the whole of our persona. When denied, they often become the stage directors of our lives re-enacting the same play with a different script over and over again.

These lives are held down beneath fate's dreary thumb—trapped in the same consciousness we abandoned them with.

The same child with all its hurts and rejections, cries to be heard, cries for love. It roams the astral world—overwhelmed—living again the denials of its parents, reliving its shock. This inner abused child will never learn to trust. S/he will live on within us, seeing the world as if all the people in it were going to hurt her/him. Inwardly s/he will live out the pattern of being unloved—reliving rejection, abandonment and abuse. Although love is what s/he needs the most, her/his outward behaviour pushes it away. This adult child is frozen in the reality of being unloved, and will recreate the pattern of rejection in outer reality.

Loss of volition in childhood is a *stressor* that causes a deep anxiety we will carry into our adult years. It makes us perpetual victims.

Lack of self-esteem, feelings that we are of no value, feelings of guilt and self-hatred are unloved parts of ourselves that twist reality into ugly shapes.

The teenager—part child, part adult, with all its insecurities continues to wear its persona like armour. The persona has become a defence, a way of preventing the world from seeing the vulnerable places—the sore and weeping wounds hidden behind psychic chain mail.

We needed to build that armour. We needed to hide our frightened little selves behind the strongest fortress we were capable of constructing. It needed to be an outer image the world could not see through. However, when the inner teenager continues to be concerned about its popularity and continues to pour its creative energy into supporting its defence mechanisms, an otherwise creative thirst for challenge and experience remains parched. This defensive nature has become another *negative coping mechanism*. The personality is maladjusted. The individual drives love away.

The inner teenager remains caught up in its presentation of itself to the outer world. It continues to hide behind walls that, as adults, we need to dismantle. Adults need to learn to show vulnerability. This, however, is the opposite of what we are taught. Society reinforces the idea of denial. It teaches us not to cry, or to show emotion. In effect, we are taught not to be real. The teenager slips into adulthood and thus engages in keeping up appearances.

However, the inner teenager still feels resentment against society's molding hand—and still wants to kick back.

We are adults in states of unconscious rebellion rather than conscious transformation.

And the young and budding male energy within the female, the young and blooming female energy within the male is stunted, its growth arrested by an avalanche of conditioning and further denials. Potential creativity is distorted into self-destruction. The thwarted will seethes. Frustration is transformed into self-hatred. Confidence becomes a mask put on in the morning in order to face the world. Love cannot find its way in past the armour. Neither can it find its way out towards a world that will mock and reject. The hidden seeds of destiny remain dormant. The inner teenager remains immature. The contra-sexual masculine and feminine aspects of our natures remain undeveloped.

Relationships continue to go wrong.

The mother also lives on within the psyche with her denials. The father too. And all the ancestors live in the psychic DNA of the blood in thoughtforms created out of astral stuff. Memories of their past deeds live on in undifferentiated guilt. Again and again, they act out their dramas eternally repeating the unresolved. Whilst we, now adults, repeat their same pattern of denial and shut our ears to their internal cries for liberation.

Awakening to our denial means we must *re-parent* the inner child. We do this by allowing the inner child to feel its pain—to cry it out, to express what could not be expressed in childhood. All the areas where the child has been made impotent must be given recognition with our adult consciousness.

Revisiting childhood after the passage of time shines new light on old issues. Unresolved hurts can now be resolved—childhood events shrunk to perspective. Its truth told—the inner child feels heard. For the first time, its reality is not denied. Thus the inner child emotionally catches up and gradually constructs a sense of personal volition that was raped all those years ago.

Six

A Date with Synchronicity

Poltergeists draw their energy from our denials. They attract chaos into our lives. They draw unhealthy relationships—inviting emotional disorder of like kind. They become saboteurs tampering with events and physical objects. They make the car break down. They make us lose our keys. They break into the computer. And they make us sick. They want us to pay them attention. They cause accidents, taking serious measures that will force us into immobility, so that we have to listen.

Synchronicity is the science that links these denied or unconscious inner events with outer ones. This does not mean that one thing causes another. Rather, energies that are similar cluster together. Like attracts like.

Three dramatic synchronistic events were to awaken me to the power of the forces of the underworld:

One afternoon, a huge black dog appeared in my garden. From my vantage-point, looking out of an upstairs window, he felt like an intruder. There was something about his appearance that terrified me. His ugly enormity was profound. It put me in mind of the mythological dog Cerberus that was said to guard the gates of Hades. The emotional charge generated in me by the sudden appearance of this dog heralded an unconscious playing out of an inner event. I was compelled to confront the scene.

I went out into the garden, but the dog was nowhere to be seen. Turning around, however, about to go back inside the house, I saw him. He was sitting looking at me from the coal shed. He had disappeared into its darkness. I was level with him, backed against a wall. It was as if he had eerily planned this, and now I had no escape. Quite suddenly, he lunged at me. His huge paws were on my shoulders knocking me down. But, surprisingly, he carried on

25

past me, pushing open the door of the kitchen with his enormous snout.

I had expected him to attack me. Instead of which he was invading my house, uninvited and unafraid. I followed him in. He was lying at the foot of my rocking chair, which had been my mother's. He did not move, but began howling. It was a chilling sound. I tried to go upstairs to get away from the nauseating pitch, but he would not let me go. He bounded in front of the door, and sat looking at me with his bloodshot eyes.

He was trying to tell me something.

My shadow had sent its emissary. It had drawn the dog, possessed it, and made it carry out a greater will. It had drawn me to the window and down the stairs; just as I had been drawn down the stairs to meet my fate that first time, long ago. My intense emotional response to the invader was an indication that somewhere within me, I already knew what it meant.

I was being shown that a great and overwhelming force was about to descend on me and knock me down. I would not be able to escape. It would invade my home, inner and outer, and make me look upon its ugliness, which was also my own. The howling warned me that hell was about to break loose. The incident left me with a sense of foreboding.

Three days later, I returned home to find my black pearls lying on the bedroom floor. I went to put them back on their chain in the jewellery box kept in my bedside drawer. But the chain was not in the jewellery box. Neither were any of the other gold chains given me by my husband.

Later that day, he returned home and was sitting facing me. I sat with my back to the window. He asked me what had happened to the window. I turned to look. The window catch was broken. There were fingerprints smudged all over it. We had been burgled. All the gold chains—gifts from him—had been stolen. Nothing else had been taken.

This was the second warning from my unconscious. The chains my husband had given me were golden. But they were still chains. I was a prisoner, chained to a negative relationship. The divine robber—who was my own soul—had attracted the physical thief to carry out the physical deed. My soul was to release me from the chains that bound me. And it would do so by force—by breaking and entering.

Synchronistic events often come in clusters. They are *meaningful coincidences.* The North American Indians used to read the signs of nature in order to interpret spiritual reality. Likewise, in our own culture, we used to believe in omens. Unfortunately, in present day western culture these beliefs are dismissed as being nothing more than superstition.

I knew these events were portents of something about to unfold.

The third dramatic event took place on the very day my husband left. No sooner had he driven away to claim his new life, than the kitchen ceiling came crashing down beside where I stood.

This was the third warning. The sky was about to fall. My place of nourishment was about to be destroyed. My home was wrecked, just as my mother's had been over and over again by my father's violence. My domestic illusion of happiness had collapsed around me.

These events happened within a week of each other. Often people experience synchronistic events when they are about to go through major changes in life style, or are about to pass through a time of extreme emotional and mental crisis. We may be blighted by disease, the break-up of a marriage, the death of a loved one, or the death of some aspect of self that gets in the way of the soul's desire to express itself. Sometimes disguised as the mid-life crisis, but long time known to the early Viking Rune makers as *Hagalaz*, it is a time when the elemental forces of the underworld are unleashed and manifest in all their power and drama.

Following those three synchronistic events, I had a prophetic dream that would prepare me for all that was to follow:

I was in the house of my soul. It was a cottage by the sea. I had been called back there from the healing I had been "out" doing. The call came from an invisible, yet absolutely superior force. Suddenly a storm blew. The winds howled and raged and beat on the windows. The rain was a battering ram besieging my door. I tried with all my puny might to bolt the door against the elemental raging of the storm. The more I tried, the angrier blew the storm. It called out to me to leave my cottage and go down to the ocean to meet it. If I did not, it would destroy my house. Though terrified, I did as I was bidden.

As I approached the beach, a tidal wave rose out of the ocean. It was a wall of thundering, crashing power. I stood in terror, unable to move. Then I noticed that the wave was peaked by a horse's head. Its mass had become the snow-white body of a stallion. Its hooves were about to pound down and crush me.

It was the giant rider at the helm of an ocean of light. All the waves that made up its vanguard were of pure white stallions frothing and foaming and stampeding all before them. My terror turned to awe, then to admiration. The stallion's power was magnificent. Its beauty alone had power enough to tear me apart with heart-wrenching yearning. I was helpless to do anything other than stand in silent praise. Just then, in the moment of recognition and surrender to my impending doom, a beam of light flashed from my brow and pierced the great stallion between the eyes. There was a flashing forth of recognition. It knew me. Its hooves arrested. The magical horn of the unicorn flashed forth from the brow of the stallion and pierced my heart.

The unicorn receded into the foam from whence he came leaving a carpet of white flowers everywhere he had been.

The unconscious is full of rich paradox. Prophetic dreams weave in and out of parallel dimensions. In one dimension, the dream may appear negative, foretelling loss and destruction and raising our worst fears to reality. That same dream, in another dimension may indicate deep and life-changing transformation. Dreams indicate not only psychic reality but also physical reality. Though the giant stallion was a manifestation of my own denied spirit, it also represented the full power of outer circumstances that were threatening to crash down on me.

My psyche was showing me what I would have to pass through in the next few years. Like torturers, shadows of the past would be churned up out of the depths of my unconscious. They would come to taunt me. Titanic forces of the unconscious that I thought were buried in some deep and secret place would again have the power to reduce me to the impotence of childhood. I would have to surrender to my vulnerability. Only my surrender to the power of the unconscious would take me through the next phase of my life. Otherwise, as indicated by the dream, I would be destroyed.

When recognised for what it is, this time of crisis can lead to spiritual initiation. The soul blows the crushing winds of involuntary change upon us. Howling winds sent by the gods of the underworld are ridden by the unlived lives of destiny. These ancient riders on their mighty steeds stampede the fragile veils that separate the worlds. And together they have the power to burst through the banks of unconsciousness leaving a trail of devastation in their wake. What may have formally been but a distant urging, now confronts us with full demand. For these are the lives of our ancestors, held in purgatory throughout the ages, now demanding resolution and release.

These unlived lives of destiny are our ancestral inheritance. Not only are they bloodline potentials that have yet to be fulfilled, they are the unresolved sins of the fathers being visited upon future generations.

Although on the surface I was nothing like my father, in running away from his violence, I had denied the violence inherent in my own spirit. This was a bloodline issue which needed resolution.

The soul is the timekeeper of Hagalaz. It stirs the sleeping monster from the depths of the unconscious. Hagalaz arises—disrupter god—inner force of nature at its most violent, and brings with it the destruction of old crystallised patterns and outworn emotional props. He knocks the crutches out from under us and bids us stand alone.

He is the reshaper of lives. He does not crush us. He tempers the blade of spirit if we give him recognition.

He is the mighty Hagalaz—harbinger of light and magical beast of transformation.

Seven

The CDan in the hill

The Tor, Glastonbury, England...

Glastonbury—known as the ancient site of the Isle of Avalon, is a source of mystical intrigue to many. Its history possibly dates as far back as twelve thousand years.

When I went there, however, I knew little of its myths or legends.

Originally surrounded by water, Avalon was an island unto itself. Gradually the waters receded and the land was reclaimed.

The site consists of a great conical hill, named the Tor, and its softly rounded feminine mate—the Chalice Hill.

The Tor has a sudden presence—jutting its attendance into the Glastonbury skies. Pilgrims, wide-eyed to their mystical past make its long ascent. Along a seven-tiered labyrinth, cut into the side of the hill, seekers of the knowledge tread the way. The path moves like a snake of wisdom twisting its way in spirals from the base of the hill to the crown. From the summit of the Tor, pilgrims have an eagle's view, as the three hundred and sixty-degree vista of the surrounding county of Somerset reaches out its green fingers to touch the circular horizon.

I climbed the Tor a token pilgrim. That English November day was cold.

I stood on the summit, gazing out across the tailored farmer's fields to the Mendip Hills in the distance. The sky was heavy. It tumbled and fell into the valleys and spread a veil of mist across the countryside.

Magic—the divine thief—crept upon me and stole away my tiredness. I was brilliantly awake and intensely alive.

Time—no longer my master—stilled and paused between its breaths.

Thoughtforms of Ancients, who had lived in ages past, had been held there in a crystal moment—nurtured by time—waiting to be plucked from the ethers.

The pregnant air sparked and cracked and burst into myriads of their tiny lives.

I heard the calling of abandoned souls carried on the high pitched voices of the winds. They called out for recognition and redemption. They bid me journey in spirit into the darkness of the long forgotten realm beneath the Tor. There would I find their salvation.

I began to feel an intense sense of destiny. Deep within me, a buried urge, long ago abandoned, began to reawaken.

I had pierced through the veil separating the worlds. I was *seeing* through the Tor into underground streams and caverns.

Commanded by an invisible presence, I entered the inner landscape...

A boat waited as if I had been expected.

Once embarked, I was guided to another shore by an invisible hand. Once there, I disembarked, and was engulfed in pitch-black darkness.

I began to climb. I knew I was beneath the Chalice Hill. My hands followed the sides of the walls that curved and fell away suddenly. The tunnel was narrow. Water dripped and cried its way along my path and hurried back to its source. I felt unstable, as my hands would slip from their stony guide.

I found myself standing beside a waterfall. The pull of the water was very strong. I knew I must resist it and enter the narrow passage that seemed to burrow into the very heart of the hill. The atmosphere in the tunnel was stifling. I could see a dim blue point of light in the distance. It was an ineffable guide drawing me onwards.

I found myself inside a tomb.
The light had swelled into a softly shimmering aura that surrounded
a sarcophagus.

An atmosphere of absolute peace and sanctity pervaded. The at-
mosphere was somehow familiar.

An unseen hand opened the lid of the sarcophagus.
A man, perfect and holy, lay as if he merely slept.
I knew, someday, he would reawaken.

His cheeks were still rosy.
He wore heavily embossed gowns.
An inner voice said they were the gowns of a rich merchant.
On his left hand he wore a ring with a large red stone in it.
The stone seemed important.
In his other hand, he held a parchment.

A voice deep inside me said, "This ring is the Royal Seal of the
House of David. The parchment he holds to his breast contains the
Legacy of Christ. When the hill shall be split asunder and give up
its find, he shall be seen to be whole, uncorrupted by time, and will
change the world forever."

I heard those words inside my own heart. I was filled with them.
They reverberated in the depths of my soul. I spilled over with
them.

I cried out, "Are these the words suffering humanity has waited so
long to hear, so long that our minds have become closed to mira-
cles, and our hearts have turned to stone?"

The light was gone. I felt a rushing sensation. I was back on the summit
of the Tor on hands and knees.

The wind had fallen. The mists had cleared.

And I went away as one cast from the world of humankind, carrying my
vision in my aching heart.

Eight

Λ Spiritual Partnership

Findhorn, North East Scotland,
November 1986...

I visited Findhorn. At the time, I had no idea that I was about to meet the man who would become my spiritual partner and who would, three years later, accompany me into the forest and witness the meeting with the angel.

Findhorn is a non-religious spiritual community situated on the North East Coast of Scotland. Its mission is to promote world peace and harmony through individual personal development. Founded by Eileen and Peter Caddy and Dorothy Maclean in the mid-sixties, it is now a well-known spiritual centre and educational trust. When I met Douglas, he was a returning Findhorn member.

Born in Canada, Douglas studied Agriculture at McGill University in Montreal. His parents were avid gardeners and were ecologists long before ecology became a popular issue. He had spent every summer of his youth exploring the untamed wilderness of the Quebec landscape.

Douglas' spiritual quest grew out of a deep desire to understand and harmonise man's relationship to nature. His liberal Protestant background imposed little religious dogma, while his father's passion for science and empirical knowledge influenced his perspective on life and his approach to learning. The fundamental split between scientific thinking and spirituality that existed in society became an inner personal dilemma for him. Although he had a science background, he had also been influenced by Rudolf Steiner's approach to organic gardening and farming.

In those early days, Findhorn had offered Douglas an environment in which people were learning how to integrate spirit with nature. The community was filled with the energy of experimentation. It had vitality and was an inspiration. He first joined the community in nineteen seventy-six. When I met him, it was his third stay at Findhorn.

He had returned to Findhorn from Africa in order to recover his health after a bout of malaria. He had been working in Southern Sudan as the Agricultural Adviser to Oxfam. He had been running an emergency mass vaccination programme for cattle suffering an epidemic of rinderpest. This was very difficult to operate due to the dangers and insecurities of civil war. Douglas lived in the villages and cattle camps out in the middle of the Southern Sudanese savannah. A tribe of Mundari had adopted him in recognition of the work he had done with them. He was completely immersed in this life with the local people whom he loved and learned from. He realised that though they were surrounded by poverty in terms of the western value system, they were rich in humanity and culture.

Being nomadic, they were not attached to possessions. However, social lives were complex. Births, deaths, marriages and initiations into adulthood were deeply embedded in tradition and ceremony. Tradition seemed to anchor the community. Everyone knew her or his place. This bred a sense of belonging. It bred security and integrity strong enough to help them confront even death from recurring famine and disease.

Douglas believes that good development work in any community depends on not imposing outside ideas, but encouraging self-empowerment. It requires respect, humility and understanding. It does not require, as is often the case, a missionary zeal that seeks to educate the poor black people who are in need of charity!

Since that time, Douglas and I returned to Africa together—both of us to work for Unicef and Oxfam. Douglas' work took him to some of the most troubled hot-spots in the world—back to war-torn Sudan, to Liberia and to Bosnia as Relief Programme Coordinator.

During that first time in Africa, however, Douglas realised how important was a sense of community.

Findhorn offered him a community as well as support for his spiritual quest. For him, this meant learning how to bring together his rational being with his feeling being. It seemed to him that these two functions were polarised in western society. In the early days, Findhorn had offered him the opportunity to attempt to unite these often seeming contradictory parts of self.

By the time I met Douglas, he felt, however, that for him, the magic had gone out of Findhorn. Because I was a non-member, the community would not allow me to stay. This meant that either I would have to become a member, or we would have to leave. We decided on the latter. Douglas invited me to Canada. My recounting of the vision of the *Man in the Hill* inspired him. He too felt its authenticity, its power and its compelling mystery.

Myself, my daughter and Douglas were about to embark on an incredible spiritual adventure.

We would unveil the mystery of the *Man in the Hill* held secret for thousands of years.

cNine

Iniciacion

The quiet voice,
Redeemer of Shadow,
called my heart to its awakening.

The West Coast of Canada was to be our home for three years. We lived in a wooden house on five acres of land, forested with giant firs and arbutus. Our garden wilderness was our sanctuary.

Alone all day with nature, I opened my heart and began to cry. I cried out my childhood. I cried out my mother's untimely and tragic death. I cried out my father—for his death and his tortured spirit. I cried for my daughter having been robbed of her father. I cried for myself.

And I felt the suffering of humanity and cried for the world.

I was awakening to the pain that had been stored in my being since the dawn of my childhood. I could not move forward until I had released the pain in my body. Every muscle, joint and vital organ remembered.

Crying is essential to the healing process. It opens our hearts. It is not self-indulgent. It is shedding—essential in the process of initiation. *Conscious crying* frees psychic energy that has been trapped in our bodies. We realise how we have lived our parent's lives—shaped by convention, compromise and expectation.

The secrets of initiation are difficult to reveal. When the soul begins to overlight and take control of the personality, it brings us to a point of spiritual crisis. The crisis is one of longing for something lost—perhaps never yet experienced. We can resist the longing. We can hide from the aching emptiness that has been stirred. Or we can accept it and pass through the inevitable disruption that follows in its wake.

So often, when disruptive, painful events happen in our lives they are ignored. However, these are rites of passage—times when it is possible to reach far enough down into *Self* to extract the deeper meaning of loss, grief, rejection, abandonment and despair.

In all our cultures and mythologies, there are stories of initiation that mark our passages of growth, or expansions of consciousness. Recounting the various demands made on spiritual warriors, they all tell of very difficult tests posed in order that *neophytes* should emerge victorious, proven able to take on greater spiritual responsibility.

Initiation has always been associated with undergoing some ordeal in order to expand our knowledge and power. This is not worldly power or political power. It is the power of *self-knowledge*. It is character making. It unfolds the flower of virtue. It gives us a deep sense of integrity and re-focuses the will.

Initiation always involves a descent into darkness. In Egyptian times, the neophyte was placed in a casket and buried alive for three days and three nights. Blanketed thus in the pitch black, the suffocating earth above, the would-be Initiate was forced to face her/himself.

The shadows and fears would come to call, and taunting then, they danced and swirled and gripped the heart. And death hovered, always close in front of the face, ready to take possession of the neophyte if s/he should panic, or lose control. If s/he emerged from this torment alive, s/he was sumptuously feasted and allowed into the *inner sanctum* where, having proved her/himself worthy, s/he would become privy to the sacred mysteries.

Spiritual initiation is always a painful process. It feels like a death. Only those souls who are called to the task will enter the underworld. The ego will be tempered. Extreme emotional and mental crisis usually inspires such a need.

We learn to live empty—in a wasteland—without purpose or will. All that we once believed in and fought for lies discarded as empty husks on the road behind us. It is a road well trodden and familiar upon which much of life's energy has been expended. But it leads nowhere. There are no new signposts. All directions are tried and used up. And the gods of the road and the sacred cows are downed and lie bespattered in the mud. Alongside which, former dreams and illusions dissolve in bitter realisation.

There are many levels of initiation. Some will experience it more deeply than others. But all of us must accept the rites of passage that lead to the portal of spiritual adulthood. If we accept the challenge of our souls, we begin to transform personal desire into *aspiration.*

We may feel the need to withdraw from the world, from its distractions and attractions. We cease to be driven by desires that lead us into the woods of bewilderment and further away from our own Inner Light.

Religious practices and dogmas teach us to fight desires, to deny and subjugate them. This is dangerous practice—a rejection of life. Desire is life's first great teacher. It demands our attention. This teacher's unfulfilled demands and secret wishes urge us to touch and taste the richness of life's full experience. Even one of desire's ungratified passions still lurking in our hearts has the power to undermine and defeat us. If we deny it, trying to fight it with our wills, it will become distorted, more powerful and destructive. It will rob us of our strength and reason. It will always sabotage good intentions. Desire urges we live it out with energy and passion.

Spiritual initiation comes when the objects of our desire fail to satisfy. We have reached a crossroads. The signpost says: *"There must be more to life than this."*

In experiencing desire, we begin to see its nature…

Deep in the woods of bewilderment, in the misty vales of the astral world, desire runs quickly after the beautiful, shimmering things that live there. They are the *glamours* who play hide and seek with desire. Shining will-o-the-wisps of illusion, they disappear as soon as desire approaches them. Desire never sees the true form of that which he pursues.

Glamours are veils that mask the truth. They dress the false persona. These filmy silken scarves cover the nakedness of the things that lurk beneath them.

When the light of the soul begins to shine, its rays penetrate deep into the mists, stirring the glamours and revealing their hidden shadows. We see them scurrying away into their dense places of hiding, as shadows do when a light is struck in a darkened room. But the light of the soul grows ever brighter until it ferrets them out. One by one the shadows fade, leaving the glamours standing revealed in the light of the inner sun. At last, we are able to see them for what they truly are—addictions that have kept us bound in unholy chaotic inner dances. Dancing like a Dervish who has lost his focus, desire spins as if one of his feet were nailed to the floor. Glamours keep him giddy. And they keep us in darkness.

Seeing through illusion makes it possible for the sacred to be revealed. We begin to know truth from falsity. It is the destiny of some of us to be called by an inner voice—called by the desire to serve something greater than the individual self. Our will re-focuses—away from the exterior, material rewards the world has to offer. We are called to discover a deeper identity—the inner life—the life of the soul.

The path of service is the path of the *aspirant.* Nothing tempers the ego more acutely than aspiring to truly serve another—whether it is a cause, a group of people, or an individual. If love is stronger in us than pride, we reach beyond ourselves. We grow in spirit. We express the soul.

Love and service pave the way of spiritual initiation. We hear its call when we have used up every other possibility that the material world has to offer. Yet none of the offerings of the material world have succeeded in nourishing the spirit or satisfying its quest.

Book Two

The Myth Makers

Ten

Amrita

The vision of the *man in the hill* had fired me with a spiritual quest of my own. The quality of his energy had stayed with me—mysterious, numinous, beckoning.

Still, I did not know his identity. Two years passed. Then knowledge came, unsought.

One day, a friend called to my house. She left a pamphlet on the "Chalice Well." It had come from Glastonbury. It fell open on page fourteen. The heading read, *The Prophesy of Melkin*. It stated the words of Maelgwn "who was before Merlin" attributed to him circa 450 AD. It said:

> *The Isle of Avalon...received thousands of sleepers amongst them Joseph De Marmore from Arimathea by name entered his perpetual sleep. He lies in the bifurcated line next the southern angle of the oratory made of Wattles...Joseph had with him moreover in his sarcophagus two white and silver cruets filled with the Blood and Sweat of the Prophet Jesus. When his sarcophagus shall be opened it will be seen whole and untouched in the future, and will be open to the whole world. From then neither water nor dew of heaven shall fail those inhabiting this most notable island.*

These words were nearly identical to those I had heard the day I climbed the Tor. Again, I was filled with their emotional power, and with the name *Joseph of Arimathea*. I spoke his name to my partner who urged the question: "Who was Joseph of Arimathea? What did he do?"

45

The answer came from some long-forgotten, once dimly perceived child-hood image of Biblical text; *"Joseph took the body of Christ down from the cross."*

I realised the symbolic meaning of Joseph's action—*He took the body of Christ down from the cross of suffering.* In so doing, he had left a message of hope for the coming age. Joseph's role in the unfolding of the Legacy of Christ was becoming more important than history has ever allowed.

The room filled with undulating power—vibrating, humming and tangible. A *Presence* was in me and around me. Words took shape out of the light that was in my heart:

> *I am the voice of the compassionate man*
> *who dwells at the heart of the feminine world.*
> *When I speak,*
> *I radiate such quality and virtue*
> *that you are filled with that light.*
> *In that light I am present.*
> *I nurture all that is pure and true.*
> *I am the scourge of all that is dark and defiled.*
> *None can be in my presence who deceive themselves.*
> *You shall know me by the name, Amrita.*

In Sanskrit, the name *Amrita* means ambrosia for the gods. I now know it to be knowledge direct from spirit—spirit-knowledge of the heart.

Amrita had revealed itself as the *Great Being* that had overlighted me that day on the Tor and inspired the vision of Joseph.

This was the same Great Spirit who had also guided Joseph in his myth-making, when he brought the Grail Chalice containing the Blood of Christ to Britain.

Amrita was the *spirit* of the Chalice.

Amrita had alluded to one of the motifs depicted in the Grail myth—only those who were pure in heart could be in the presence of the Grail.

Many knights had tried to gain it. Galahad died when he looked upon it. Lancelot was blinded by his own guilt and grief reflected back to him by the purity of the Chalice. Only Parsifal, the most foolish of all the knights, was eventually successful.

Eleven

Following Terrestrial Signs

Though Joseph's tale begins the weaving of the Grail adventure, the mystery of Glastonbury began millennia before Joseph—millennia before the advent of druids—when a race of men came to Britain, knowledgeable enough in the sacred sciences to have created a *terrestrial zodiac.*

Out of earth mounds, watercourses, rivers, earthworks, roads, hills and footpaths, they constructed a *replica zodiac*—shaped out of the natural features of the land. This phenomenon is known as the *Glastonbury Zodiac.*

It was discovered in the mid 1920's by Catherine Maltwood—inspired while studying large scale maps of the countryside surrounding the Tor.

The *terrestrial zodiac* is of particular interest to many different research-ers. Each sign naturally crafted in the Glastonbury landscape, tallies precisely with its corresponding star constellation that shines so far above.

Amrita revealed to me how the ancient masters of wisdom achieved this. They knew the secrets of *thought-building.*

They created *forms* in which their thoughts could live—out of *etheric, astral* and *mental* energy. Then projecting them onto the Glastonbury landscape, they simply waited.

And the land took shape around them, giving physical form to the heavenly zodiac.

Thus the English countryside was engraved by *thoughtforms* of Ancients.

It was a legacy for those who would follow after.

Twelve

The Psychic Wounding
of an Age

After Joseph had taken the body of Christ down from the cross, Christ's wounds began to bleed anew. Joseph caught the drops of blood in the Chalice that had been used for the Last Supper. He wrapped Him in a linen shroud and laid Him in his family sepulchre.

The body of Christ disappeared from the tomb. Joseph was imprisoned, blamed for its disappearance.

In his solitude, Christ appeared to him and gave the Chalice back into his keeping. He revealed that the Chalice contained the *three persons of the one godhead. The three powers that are one and the blessed woman would give him counsel.* He would hear that counsel in his own heart.

Guided by the voice of the Holy Spirit, he brought the sacred Chalice containing the Legacy of Christ to Britain.

Joseph came to Avalon.

Significantly, he is said to have planted his staff on Wearyall Hill. Out of his staff grew a holy thorn. To this day, the thorn bush still flourishes at Glastonbury. It is a genuine Levantine variety and is grown nowhere else in England.

Wearyall Hill is one of the natural land features that comprise Glastonbury's terrestrial zodiacal sign of Pisces.

Amrita revealed to me the profound mystical significance of Joseph's legendary act:

> *The planting of the staff on Wearyall Hill*
> *signified the inception of the Age of Pisces.*

Christianity would take root in England.

Out of Joseph's staff grew a holy thorn,
symbol of the crown of thorns,
symbol of the age of suffering that was about to come.

Two fish allegorise Pisces.
They are devotion and desire,
swimming in different directions,
food for different lords.

One fish is the soul,
the other is the shadow it casts upon the earth.
Man is the shadow cast by the soul upon the earth.

Christ, Fisher of the Soul,
Illuminator of Shadows,
Redeemer of Selfish Desire,
God made Wo-man,
Wo-man made God,
Embodiment of Soul and Shadow Reconciled;
through whose crucifixion,
entered the shadow world
and cast His reflection upon the waters of the earth.

It was the net into which many fish would swim.

Caught in His reflection,
wo-men saw a wounded fisher king,
crowned with thorns,
a shadow Christ
reflected in the waters of emotion.
He became the wounded spirit of sacrifice,
the martyred spirit of Pisces,
the king who could not rule,
whose kingdom would never grow green again.

The two fish swam in different directions.
And the dual nature of wo-man rent the human will asunder
and shackled humanity to a shadow cross.
Christ's reflection suffers on within each one.
His kingdom is laid waste, infertile,

*until one should come who will take him down from the
cross of suffering
and reveal the true nature of Christ.*

Amrita had revealed the psychic wounding of an Age.

This is an inherited psychic wounding that has condemned the Christian
world to live beneath the shadow of the cross.

The Wounded Fisher King is an archetype. He is a metaphor for the
spirit of Christianity. I saw him in the eyes of those around me. I saw
him depicted in our religions—not as the risen Christ teaching us through
His actions the symbolic meaning of sacrifice, which means transformation—but absorbed into our collective psyches, by our emotional response
to the macabre.

We are wounded in spirit. Our image of Christ is distorted—a parody of
the real spirit.

Emotionally, we respond to a crucified Christ, not the living Christ! We
do not know Christ within our own hearts. We know only self-sacrifice,
self-denial, guilt and grief. He lives on, in the collective psyche, in shadow
form, turned into a *wounded fisher king* who perpetually suffers for our
sins.

This collective psychic wounding is a recurring motif reflected in many
of our western cultural myths.

Amrita inspired me to integrate these myths into a creative synthesis.
They needed to be interpreted collectively in order that their psychic
meaning became clear.

The integrated tale of the Fisher King:

> One day, the Fisher King rode out, filled with his youth, and with
> the joy of amorous intent. A lance dripping blood came hurtling at
> him with such force, he was knocked to the ground. It pierced his
> thigh and cost him his manhood. He was given a wooden leg to
> remind him of the cross upon which Christ died for him. Limita-
> tion became his teacher. Thus fettered, he could never again run
> forward of his own volition to pursue the sudden rush of his desire,

but drag the heavy weight of wood behind him as if it were a shadow cross.

The wound never healed. His suffering was unbearable. The wound robbed him of his power. His energy was used, fighting the eternal fight with desires he could not fulfil. Still they rage within him. Yet none can free him of them or heal him.

Only the tip of the same spear that wounds, the same hurt inflicted again into the wound can ease his suffering.

The motif of the spear that drips blood appears in Parsifal's tale. During his Grail adventures, Parsifal had come to the castle wherein the Grail was kept—although he did not realise its significance or value. After a strange evening's entertainment, he witnessed a procession in which bizarre people and objects were paraded in front of him. One of these objects was a lance dripping blood. But Parsifal had failed to question its meaning. Instead he had got drunk on the wine and had fallen asleep.

Amrita illuminated me on the *psychic* significance of the spear that drips blood.

> *The spear comes from the world of shadows.*
> *It is the spear of inspiration,*
> *an arrow of love,*
> *thrown from a great distance,*
> *delivered with such force*
> *as to influence an age.*
>
> *It is the shadow of the centurion's spear*
> *that struck the side of Christ*
> *as He died on the cross.*
> *None can see the hand that hurls it,*
> *or the deep wound it inflicts.*
>
> *Some of Christ's Blood remained on its tip.*
> *When it struck the young king,*
> *the Blood of Christ entered his veins.*
> *He became the king of the struggling conscience,*
> *ruler of the age of Pisces.*

He is the wounded spirit,
wounded by the Blood of Christ,
destined to carry world suffering.
Upon his fragile shoulders,
he bears world ignorance.
He is bowed beneath the weight of it.
It is the heaviest cross in the world.

He is crucified by victims and torturers,
by violent ones who strike out of anguish,
and destroy out of hate.
He is rendered impotent by their suffering.
He is the victim of the anguish they deny.

It is the anguish of loneliness and rejection,
of abandonment, fear and loss.
It is a dark and festering wound that will not heal
except by the power of love.

It crucifies him on the shadow cross.
Again, he feels the searing agony of the lance
piercing him with the highest human ideals.
He has aspired to serve those ideals
throughout the age of Pisces.

He is the wounded fisher king
wounded by the Blood of Christ.
He will not be free until his redeemer comes.
He languishes,
He bleeds,
He longs for redemption.
Let Christ inflict His spear again.
Only the Blood of Christ can release his wounded spirit.

Amrita had revealed to me how the Fisher King was a pagan king wounded by the Blood of Christ.

I found the spectre of the Wounded Fisher King within my own heart and soul. I felt his anguish and loosed his cries for redemption. I too had been pierced by the highest human ideals. The Blood of Christ had entered my psychic veins.

My vision had revealed Joseph wearing a ring, which I was told, was the *Royal Seal of the House of David*. This meant that he was of the direct *Bloodline* of Christ. At the time I had the vision, there was little public knowledge of who Joseph was. It has since been researched and suggested that he may have been Christ's great-uncle or even his brother. I could not have known this.

Amrita had revealed this truth in a vision to someone with an open heart, completely unversed and, therefore, untainted by history or academic foreknowledge. There had been such feeling, power and astoundingly accurate detail attached to those images I had received that cold November day on the Tor. They would burn inside me, urging understanding.

I had visioned the man in the hill wearing lavishly embossed gowns. In the vision, I had been told these were the gowns of a rich merchant. Again, at the time of the vision, there was no public knowledge that Joseph may have been a tin merchant, originally come to Britain to trade with Cornwall's mines.

Grail legends tell us that Joseph was the *grandfather* of Alain Li Gros who was the father of Parsifal.

My vision had revealed Joseph holding a parchment, which I was told, was the *Legacy of Christ*. It was the *uncorrupted Word of Christ*—the legacy of the soul's knowledge passed down the ages.

Joseph is the psychic embodiment of Christ's legacy. He continues Christ's history. His task is to pass it to the son of his son, through the ancestral *spiritual* bloodline to us, the Parsifals of our own time.

Joseph's blood relationship to Christ was an essential clue to the revelation of the *Coming of the Feminine Christ*. Just as the Grail Chalice is not a physical object, but the spiritual legacy of the transpersonal, cabalistic Christ, so too we should not be searching for physical descendants of Christ's Bloodline.

All those wounded by the Blood of Christ are Parsifals. We are Christ's *spiritual* descendants.

Thirteen

The Mysterious Chalice

It is the dawning of the Age of the Heart.
The land itself entombs an ancient thought.

Joseph marked the inception of an Age when he planted his staff on Wearyall Hill. However, I had visioned him sleeping in the *Chalice Hill.* I had been told he would reawaken—that the *hill shall be split asunder and give up its find and he shall be seen to be whole, uncorrupted by time, and shall change the world forever.*

I realised these words signified the end of the Age of Pisces—which had inspired in us devotion and idealism—and prophesied the inception of a new golden Age—the Age of the heart.

The vision of Joseph asleep in the Chalice Hill is a prophecy for this coming age. It declares a spiritual awakening—in which we have a new task to perform. But like him, we must first take the spirit of Christ down from the cross of suffering.

Joseph was an ordinary man. He was not one of the disciples, neither was he a saint. Yet it was he who took the body of Christ down from the cross. His message to the new age dawning is one of compassion—meant for all of us ordinary wo-men. We must take our *Selves* down from the cross of guilt, self-sacrifice and denial. This is the shadow cross on which the soul of humankind is crucified. And we will only achieve this through understanding the mystery of the *Chalice.*

Amrita illuminated this mystery, and revealed to me how the Chalice in which Joseph metaphorically sleeps is an allegory for the sanctified mystical heart:

> *The chalice contains the Blood of Christ.*
> *The chalice is the heart.*
> *The heart contains the Blood of Christ.*

> *Buddha was the Christ of the East.*

57

He taught the Lotus Sutras of the Heart.
The heart is the Twelve Petalled Lotus.
The twelve petals of the lotus are twelve apostles.
Each apostle embodies
one of the virtues of the heart.

To realise the virtues of the heart
are the quests of the twelve knights
of the Round Table.
The Knights of the Round Table
represent the twelve signs of the zodiac.

In each sign, we have a task to perform
in order to gain one of the virtues of the heart.
These are the Twelve Labours of Hercules,
he who is the Son of God and the Son of Man,
the soul and shadow incarnate
seeking wholeness through failure, pain and conflict.

The Round Table is the Heart,
The Round Table is the Zodiac.
The Zodiac is the Heart of Heaven.

Esoteric Astrology attributes the myths of the Labours of Hercules to each of the signs of the Zodiac. Hercules is a Son of God and yet a Son of Man—*soul and shadow incarnate.* Thus he is a Christ figure representing divine humanity. In each sign of the Zodiac, Hercules has an immense spiritual task to perform. Each task symbolises not only an individual, but also a collective initiation—an expansion of consciousness—a lesson learned.

By the grace of *Amrita,* I had been shown how the collective initiation in the sign of Pisces implied suffering, crucifixion and polarisation; whereas the Aquarian initiation was to be a collective heart awakening. *Amrita* had revealed that Joseph embodies the spirit of the Age to come. When his truth is revealed, he would symbolise the spirit of an ordinary person who dwells at the heart and thus becomes sanctified. *Amrita* had filled me with the inspiration to describe Joseph as the *compassionate man who dwells at the heart of the feminine world.* This metaphor was to indicate the profound spiritual achievement now possible in the Aquarian Age, by which masculine and feminine spirits shall be reunifed, raised to divinity. This is the Aquarian Grail.

58

The Grail Chalice contains the Blood of Christ. Blood symbolises masculine force—spirit, power, will, bloodline, ancestry. The Chalice symbolises feminine heart—compassion, feeling and love. In this image Amrita had revealed to me the most powerful symbol of spiritual unity—the integration of feminine and masculine energies: Yin and yang, soul and spirit, earth and heaven, woman and man, feeling and thinking, sensation and intuition.

Duality is reconciled.

This theme is reflected in Glastonbury's terrestrial motif depicting Aquarius. The Tor—symbol of masculine spirit, is mate to the Chalice Hill—symbol of feminine heart.

The motif depicting the union of masculine and feminine spirits is echoed in the image that represents the Sign of Aquarius: a heavenly man pours water from a pitcher.

The pitcher depicts the *spiritual heart.* It is another allegory for the Grail Chalice. Water symbolises the soul—or psychological femininity.

Thus in the Age of Aquarius, the heavenly man shall pour forth his feminine self to nourish the parching earth. The spirit shall descend and be expressed through the feminine paradigm of feeling and meaning.

The words of Melkin: "neither water nor dew from heaven shall fail this most notable island" reflect the prophetic inception of the Age of Aquarius when it is promised that the land shall grow green again and flourish.

In these images are hidden secret reference to a sacred inner marriage referred to by alchemists as *Conjunctio*. And this is to be our spiritual achievement in the Age to come. In this consummation, the new Christ is born—not of the virgin womb, but of the pure in heart. Humanity will be forced—or inspired, to learn the science of love and relationship. This is the Aquarian ideal—to understand this inner science—the science of the heart. This is a feminine spirituality, focused in the heart. It has never yet been awakened or realised.

The collective awakening of feminine spirituality shall herald the *Second Coming—the coming of the Feminine Christ.*

The world will have to change the way it has lived for thousands of years.

Fourteen

The Feminine Christ

The Grail legend was so powerful a story, historically emerging around the twelfth century, (although there are much earlier references to it) that legends grew up around the writers of the legends.

One of these recounts how the book of the Grail was given to a celibate monk who lived in the wilds known as "White Britain." He had purified himself through fasting and prayer. He was told that this was Christ's book, written by Christ Himself.

We do not know the identity of the monk to whom Christ is said to have appeared. However, the Grail legend is distinguished from fairy tales or other myths in that the identity of some of the writers is known.

Mostly, they were scholars, poets or mystics who were said to have received direct inspiration from Christ.

Thus the Grail legend that has emerged over centuries is an unusual synthesis of myth and history, mystical and scholastic inspiration.

In my own life, I became aware of parallels to the life of that early monk, in the way that the meaning of this story was revealed to me. During my vision of the Chalice Hill, I had been told that the parchment I had seen Joseph holding contained Christ's mystical truth. Slowly this truth was being revealed to me. It felt as if *Amrita* was revealing Christ's book. And I was bidden to write it. Reluctant and innocent, I had tapped into archetypal symbols and motifs that had been handed down from generation to generation. Mystical visions preceded scholastic revelation. And all through this mystical quest, *Amrita* illuminated the meaning of this occult literature.

In the Robert de Boron version of the Grail myth, we are told that Christ spoke to Joseph of Arimathea when he was imprisoned, blamed for the disappearance of Christ's body, saying:

The enemy, who does nothing to save,
lie in wait for people to incite them to evil,
first seduced Eve
because she was weaker in spirit than man;
and because all mankind was reduced to captivity by a woman,
God desired that all should be freed by a woman.

These words literally mean that a woman is destined to embody the new Christ—although this may be an extremely unpopular idea amongst thinkers who are trapped in the masculine paradigm.

Referring back to Parsifal's adventures inside the castle of the Grail, we are told of the strange and wonderful sights that passed before him in procession. One of these was a woman carrying the Grail Chalice. Again, Parsifal did not question the meaning.

The Grail Chalice symbolises the Blood of Christ in the sanctified heart.

The Feminine Christ shall be the one who brings forth the Grail to the Aquarian Age. She shall have undergone the Heart initiation thus setting free the souls of her ancestors. She shall have atoned for the sins of the bloodline. Thus she shall have greatly strengthened her spirit. In her, duality shall have been reconciled. Her spirit shall pour forth his feminine self to nourish the spiritually parched earth. Her spirit shall be as a compassionate man who dwells at the heart of the feminine world. She shall have been sanctified by the Blood of Christ. She shall therefore be an Initiate of the mystical Bloodline of Christ. And she shall carry the true mystical teaching of the feminine god to the Aquarian Age. This is a feminine message, born of the feminine world, in which feeling and meaning create a new paradigm. And just as Joseph brought the Piscean Grail to Britain, which symbolised the awakening conscience, this woman is destined to bring forth the Aquarian Grail, which shall guide humanity in the collective awakening of the heart.

Only the awakened heart shall avert the apocalypse.

Fifteen

The Aquarian Initiate

Christ was crucified on the cross of matter in order to be reborn into the life of spirit.

The Robert de Boron version of the Grail myth tells us that after His crucifixion, Christ descended into hell and freed Adam and Eve who were His ancestors from their bondage.

Through His sacrifice, He was enabled to enter into the realm of spirit and perceive His ancestors with understanding. Thus, He freed his *bloodline.*

Every bloodline eventually produces its own saviour.

Symbolically, Christ shows us the way.

His actions bid the Parsifals among us who are of the *spiritual bloodline* of Christ to make the same descent into the darkness, or hell of our own unconscious.

This is a figurative crucifixion when the personal ego is sacrificed in order to be reborn into the life of spirit. When this happens, reality turns inside out—the personal ego becomes negative, the spirit positive.

This does not mean that the ego becomes weak or passive. It means our will is focused in the life of the soul.

We are in the physical world, but not of it. We have become Initiates of the spirit world.

The theme of death and resurrection occurs in Church beliefs and teachings. The Christian Church has appropriated this theme. For it is a recurring motif that appears in world myth and most religions.

Christian symbols have layers of meaning that has been all but lost to the western world. And just as Christian churches were built on ancient sacred sites, Christian symbols are based on much more ancient spiritual motifs. These ancient motifs sign the way to modern-day psychological development.

The crucifixion symbolises the Age of Pisces. According to the ancient wisdom teachings dating back twelve thousand years, Pisces was the great zodiacal sign destined to bring forth a saviour. And when he came, we would crucify him. The thousands of years of much older pagan ceremonies, which involved the spilling of blood, had primed our unconscious to expect our saviour to die for us.

The notion of sacrifice was ever present in our psyches. Christ was the embodiment of this idea. He came at the right time. He lived out an archetypal pattern that had been in existence in the collective unconscious for thousands of years.

He was living a greater life than his own personal identity.

The prophecy that declared Christ's Blood would save us, lives on. This notion has influenced the western psyche bringing forth such powerful emotional response so as to be the foundation upon which all our devotional institutions are built.

The prophecy has yet to be fulfilled.

There is evidence of blood rituals in practically every culture. Ritualistic spilling of blood was a sacrifice to the ancestors. It invoked an awed respect by ancient peoples for the mystery of blood. This ceremony would appease the wrath of the gods. And it would reunite the living with the souls of ancestors long dead. In the secret of the blood was the power to unite past and present and thus determine the future.

Blood was holy.

Ancient wisdom teachings pronounce the blood to be *the seat of the soul*. To the ancients, therefore, spilling of blood meant setting free the souls of the ancestors.

Perhaps the *psychic DNA* of our ancestors is literally passed to us through the physical blood. If the soul is in the blood, the essence of the person exists in the blood.

The soul is the psychic force of blood. It's the blood's vital energy.

Understanding the psychic mystery of blood is the greatest secret in esoteric healing.

In western modern-day embalming rituals the vital organs are pummelled
so that the blood can be drained from the body. The body is then filled
with formaldehyde and the blood is flushed into the sewer system! This
practice blasphemes against the sacredness of the dying process. It de-
files the spirit and desecrates the blood.

The blood sacrifice is a metaphor expressing a *spiritual* initiation. In the
Age of Aquarius, no victim shall be offered up. We are destined to in-
herit the *Legacy of Christ*. This is written in the symbols and signs of the
Glastonbury myths and landscape.

If we make the psychological journey into the underworld we experience an expansion of consciousness. We gain the gift of inner sight and
perceive the inner realms. And ghosts of the past kindle visions of the
future.

In this spirit realm our ancestors live on in *thoughtforms.*

These thoughtforms are psychic embodiments of bloodline issues. They
are relic contents of the unconscious—psychic DNA—tendencies that determine psychological reality.

These are transpersonally located *archetypes.*

These ancient thoughtforms keep the ancestral soul in purgatory.

The notion of purgatory is a relatively new concept in Christian theol-
ogy. It recognises the possibility of redemption.

In the Age of Aquarius, we have a new Herculean task to live out. The
Hercules myth in Aquarius describes this task as the *cleansing of the
Aegean stables.* For centuries, the droppings of the Aegean cattle had
piled up in the stables. Plague spread throughout the land.

Cattle represent unconscious Humanity. Their droppings are the sins of
our ancestors.

In order to complete the cleansing in one day (symbolising a lifetime),
Hercules redirected two rivers. These rivers portray feeling or soul force.
Redirected, these rivers of emotion flow through spiritual channels

situated either side of the spine. These channels are known in Sanskrit as *Ida and Pingala*. The central channel is *Sushumna* along which the sleeping serpent fire coiled at the base of the spine and known as *Kundalini* will eventually be raised up.

When this fire is raised the spiritual wo-man is perfected. Ancient psychic refuse is cleansed. The blood is charged with spiritual force and is thus purified. The third eye is illuminated. The Initiate gains the gift of *spiritual sight* and becomes a prophet, mystic or visionary.

This initiation correlates with Christ's Transfiguration on the mount. His garments were said to turn as white as snow. Moses—symbolising past knowledge, and the prophet Elijah—symbolising future knowledge, appeared there beside Him. This image signifies that the Initiate gains knowledge of the past and a vision of the future.

The raising of the Kundalini will be the spiritual achievement in Aquarius. This is the ultimate consummation of feminine with masculine, soul with spirit, earth with heaven.

Cleansing the Aegean Stables means we account for the sins of our ancestors. The ancestral soul is consequently purified in the blood that fills our own hearts. Thus the chalice is made divine—the mystical heart fully awakened.

If we are to release the Wounded Fisher King from his perpetual ancient suffering we must journey into ancestral pain. If psychic suffering is not allowed full expression, it festers away behind the locked doors of unconsciousness causing ancestral miasma—physical, psychological and societal.

We should not be afraid to journey into the underworld to account for our past. We cannot regain the knowledge and inspiration of our ancestors unless we go there.

Book Three
Voyage of a Seer

Sixteen

Mists of Avalon

At the advent of Christianity, legend has it that mists grew up around Avalon veiling it from the new Glastonbury of the priests. They thickened until they were so dense as to make them impenetrable to all except those who knew the secret rites of passage and were called to make the journey. Thus the Ancient Knowledge became hidden from all but the few, lest it be abused.

In time, the knowledge almost disappeared completely. Seekers of the knowledge who had not yet developed *conscience* entered the mists of illusion. These were *astral* mists—nothing more than glamour, seductive to those who sought spiritual power.

Now, at the turn of the Age, a new opportunity to enter the mists and claim back the long-lost knowledge presents itself…

I turned my eyes from the outer world, to look within, into my own *astral* mists of illusion. I entered into a long-abandoned inner world—peopled only with ghosts of the past. The ancestors had called me to atone for their sins. It would take strength of inner vision to fully perceive those inhabitants of the inner vales.

If I had not sufficient mental power as I entered the mists, I would become lost in them, lulled into a soporific state—as Parsifal had been when first he came to the castle of the Grail. He witnessed a strange procession pass before him, but questioned none of it. He became drunk on the wine and fell asleep.

To enter the mists of illusion, I would have to struggle to remain conscious of where I trod and what I saw. At first, all appeared as reverie—phantoms and elusive wisps that I failed to experience emotionally. I could not catch the images, nor penetrate their meaning. With practice, I developed my ability to inwardly concentrate. With no guide, other than the light of my own soul, I entered the mists to set free the souls of my ancestors.

Conscience became a bright torch with which to illuminate the inner darkness.

Initially, I did this for love of my daughter. I did not want to pass negative, unconscious ancestral traits to her. By liberating myself from the past, my daughter would also be free to pursue her own destiny.

It was necessary to withdraw from the world for a time.

Those of us who hear this call may have to leave our homes, extended families and friends. We may have to sacrifice our career and income. We may even have to sacrifice our sexuality.

Initiation requires all our energies to be intensely re-focused, inwards.

The monks of old were asked to renounce worldly things. Like them, we should only do this when we have a true calling, and then not necessarily for life—but while passing through the inner transformation. After which, it is our task to come back to the world in the spirit of service, to share the fruits of inner knowledge—to be *in the world but no longer of it.*

It is not possible for most people to withdraw from the world. Learning how to practice the *science of right relationship* in daily life amidst the noise and distractions—the financial and social pressures, is a different task no less difficult. Even so, there are many ways to retreat from the world by joining meditation, therapy and spiritual groups. But the focus of this withdrawal should be to face and acknowledge one's own denials and destructive bloodline issues.

Originally, monks were celibate that sexual energy could be redirected. They did not abstain from sex because it was deemed impure. They abstained so as to have the energy for deep prayer and meditation. They used their sexual energy to penetrate the inner world. Early mystics tell of being ravished by their own spirit, when in a state of spiritual ecstasy the full force of spirit entered them and illuminated them with sacred knowledge.

Sublimated sexual energy added strength and power to consciousness. It focused the mind and intensified the act of commitment and dedication. If the individual was not really called to this initiation, repression of desires as an act of will led to very unwholesome results.

The Church has taken the symbolic and metaphoric literally. Thus, it has lost the meaning of the ancient mysteries. It has turned them into dogma. Celibacy should not be dogmatically self-imposed for a lifetime, either individually or institutionally. We are all different. Some of us are naturally more sexual than others. Sexual energy is a spiritual force—to be celebrated. If, however, the individual is destined to become a mystic, prophet or visionary, it is necessary to practice celibacy for a time.

If sexual energy is transmuted into consciousness, it will awaken the third eye. The Initiate becomes the true *Seer*. This is a truth well understood by the Initiates of the East. This is also the ancient knowledge on which the Church originally based its celibate practices.

The illuminated third eye can be described as *a highly developed consciousness touched by divinity.*

Being a *Seer* is not the same as being psychic—which is an unconstrained reception of the emotional thoughtforms of others. Rather, the illuminated third eye gives us the ability to perceive other realities much subtler and deeper than emotional states of being.

We enter into the world of soul with the eye of the heart.

During the initiation process, the head and heart become one. They are merged in the Initiate who has learned to think with the heart and feel with the mind.

Thus, I entered into the mists and saw through illusion—and into *subtle worlds* that underlie physical reality.

The *Subtle* reality is the realm in which visionaries, mystics and poets of the soul, sojourn.

Seventeen

The Subtle Anatomy

Of individuals and planets . . .

humans and planets are much more than merely physical. We also have an unseen *Subtle Anatomy* that underlies the physical body. It is constituted of the *Aura, Etheric Body, Chakras, Astral Body, Mental, Soul and Spirit* bodies.

Knowledge of the *Subtle Anatomy* has long been buried in the mists. In the future, this esoteric science will enter into the world of academic study. Medical practitioners and psychologists will work alongside Initiates, who are able to perceive the *subtle* realities. Combining and integrating scientific skills with spiritual insight and knowledge of the Subtle Anatomy will lead to much deeper understanding of the nature of human and planetary disease.

Study of the Subtle Anatomy enables sense-making of the esoteric truth that *we are all one.* In early Christian teachings, the Collective Subtle Anatomy was referred to as the *Mystical Body of Christ.* Whilst modern New Age teachings refer to this collective body as the great *World Mother.* This planetary being is known as *Gaia:* mother of nature, sentient life of the earth. It is the planetary spiritual body to which we are all connected, yet within which we have our individual being.

Much is said about the human *Aura.* Psychics may tell you yours is blue or golden. The Aura is *never* only one Colour.

It appears to me as a cloud of vibrating energies moving at different speeds. At the centre of the cloud is the physical body. It is energy's darkest and most dense expression of itself. Like a silhouette, set in relief against its much lighter background, the physical body appears but a shadow.

Surrounding the physical body, energies—subtler by far—breathe *themselves* out. Colours flash forth and make their impression on you and me. Some can read them; most can not. All can tacitly *feel* them even if unaware of what they perceive.

Our Colours communicate all we are. In those Colours, I *see* the potential of the heart—a tiny spark, alas, not often enough the burning flame that has been fanned by spirit.

Each pulsation is a different hue. Some are beautiful—some not. I *see* the effluvium of denial—anger, fear, hurt and ugly motivations that emerge from the inner darkness. These look like the gathering of menacing storm clouds. Deep reds, greys and blacknesses swirl in an angry gavotte. Sometimes, hard jagged lines of energy will flash out with malevolent intent towards another human being.

Experiencing the world through them, they corrupt all we see, touch and hear. This energy manifests in loaded words. The dead weight of the unspoken word hangs like shock in midair. This is passive aggression—unconscious malevolent attack. More often than not, I see how totally unaware individuals are of what they do to someone else. For although thoughts can not be seen or heard, they can be felt, and are, in the long run, no less destructive than a physical attack. Into the sensitive feeling body of the victim they fly like poisoned darts, and fester into unconscious wounds that will eventually manifest misfortune.

Christ bids us to be pure in thought.

In persons who have developed a greater degree of consciousness, beautiful hues can be seen to play around them. In these persons, most of the dark clouds have been dispersed, ugly emotional patterns melted in the burning light of consciousness. The heart is open, purified, and truly alive.

A well-developed aura, however, may not necessarily be comfortable to be with. A pure heart acts as a mirror. Light shone upon us by one who is pure in heart illuminates the lurking things we do not wish to face. This is why the Grail myth imparts the wisdom that none can be in the presence of the Grail unless they are pure in heart.

*T*he *etheric body* is an intricate and beautiful design. Its delicate weblike strands interlace and form a framework of light upon which the physical body is built. Shimmering, pulsating, softly golden, it radiates about half an inch around each of us. The etheric body is the exact double of the physical one.

Subtler in density than the physical form, the etheric body interweaves inner and outer worlds. All expressions of life are linked through the etheric body of the planet. This arterial network of force reaches out to all parts of itself. With quiet efficiency no part of nature's need goes unheeded. In this way, we are each instruments of communication, able to transmit our tacit thoughts and feelings to each other.

In healing work, the initiated healer knows how to travel out along the etheric web in order to reach the person they seek to heal. If we can heal from a distance, then how much more do we harm from a distance!

The Internet or World Wide Web, is a physical manifestation of the etheric web.

*T*he etheric web has inner pathways. In *Sanskrit,* these are called the *nadis.* They appear to me like an intricate system of fibre optics. Energy from deeper sentient worlds flows into them and then into physical expression. Where energy blocks occur in the nadis, I see disease begin to manifest.

In the physical body, the nadis correlate with the sympathetic nervous system. Whilst in the planetary body, they correlate with the *Ley Lines.*

Ley lines are great lines of force that weave their way around the earth as though they were the physical veins of Mother Nature carrying within them the lifeblood of our planet. They cover the world transporting sentient life to all the parts that make up the whole planetary consciousness.

*W*here all the lines of etheric force cross, meet and intersect, energy vortexes called *Chakras* well together. Upon these sites humankind has built its holy shrines and civilisations.

At these various power points around the earth, the veil separating the subtle worlds from the physical world is thinnest and may more easily be penetrated. This is where the ancestors dwell—ever present in ancient thoughtforms. Glastonbury is one such place of power.

Just as the planet has Chakras, so too does the individual. They look like swirling vortexes tied to the spine in loose knots of Colour.

We are often told that each of the Chakras has a fixed Colour. Based mainly on the work of C.W. Leadbeater, this dogma has never been challenged. This is a simplistic interpretation of the complex nature of Colour and the Chakras. Buddhism teaches meditation on certain Colours in relation to certain Chakras. Theirs is a practice with a specific purpose and does not insinuate that the Chakras only express themselves in those fixed Colours. Where Leadbeater paints pictures of Chakras that look like funnels or trumpets with definite Colours, I perceive them as much more subtle in their expression.

The word Chakra is *Sanskrit* and means *wheel*. As our spiritual and vital energies travel from wheel to wheel, or station to station, they pick up, like passengers, the qualities of each Chakra visited along the way. Therefore, the condition of one Chakra greatly affects the next. Mixed as if on a painter's palette, the Colours emerging from deeper sentient realities are intermingled, their original quality slightly changed. Our thoughts, desires and aspirations are as station-masters, redirecting the blended energies to every part of the body. They determine the direction the Chakra wheels will turn.

There are seven major Chakras or centres situated along the spine. Each one serves a different purpose. And each one struggles to allow into being the deepest *Self*.

The *seventh* Chakra is the *crown* centre. Situated at the top of the head, this centre governs the pineal gland, the cerebral cortex, the central nervous system, and the right eye. Its quality is will. It is ruled by the father principle of power, purpose and destiny.

The *sixth* Chakra is the *brow* centre. Situated between the eyebrows, it governs the pituitary gland, the left eye, nose and ears. It is known also as the third eye. Its quality is light, illumination. It is the seat of consciousness, the ruler of the self.

The *fifth* Chakra is the *throat* centre. It governs the thyroid gland, parathyroid, hypothalamus, throat and mouth. Its quality is communication.

The *fourth* Chakra is the *heart* centre. Situated in the middle of the upper chest between the breasts, it rules the thymus gland, the heart and circulatory system, the arms and hands. Its quality is love. It is ruled by the Christ principle.

The *third* Chakra is the *solar plexus*. Situated below the ribs and above the navel, it rules the pancreas, gall bladder, nervous system and stomach. It is the seat of the emotions. The solar plexus is the emotional brain of the stomach. Its function is to digest all our emotional responses. It is the seat of the *Astral Body*.

The *second* Chakra is the *sacral centre*. Situated below the navel, it rules the ovaries, the testicles, prostrate, genitals, spleen, womb and bladder. It is the seat of our sexuality and drive to go out into the world and achieve.

The *first* Chakra is the *root*. Situated at the base of the spine. It rules the adrenals, kidneys, spinal column, colon, legs and bones. Its quality is self-preservation. It is the seat of the instincts and ruled by the mother principle of being, nurturing and survival.

The qualities inherent in each Chakra must meet the vices. These qualities and vices are remnants of archetypes that have been psychically passed down through the ages by those lives that have gone before. On a swirling battleground of force, each is made victim of the other. Thus they are held until the aspirations of the person have grown strong enough to meet the inner challenge that has been called forth by the quiet voice of the soul. Then must we turn our hitherto downward focused eyes unto the light and service of our own soul—that the soul may be the ultimate victor.

This is the struggle of the *aspirant*—the neophyte approaching initiation. At this point, it seems as if we have struggled for so long. We are weary pilgrims. Perhaps Wearyall Hill where Joseph planted his staff is aptly named! Joseph's message serves those who have been continuously disillusioned in the real search for spiritual transformation.

We are destined to become souls incarnate.

The Chakras begin a painful turn. Like great wheels, first they must slow, then momentarily pause, then commence the slow and painful turn the other way. Gradually they gather momentum and begin to radiate a greater desire than a personal one.

This is the desire for service.

This pause is an elongated moment of intense inner stillness. This is the most difficult and dangerous time in the life of the seeker. The seeker must choose between the left and the right hand path—to use knowledge gained to serve the self, or to serve the greater good.

This pause is depicted in the Grail myth. The morning after Parsifal had witnessed the strange procession pass in front of him, the castle of the Grail mysteriously disappeared. A most loathsome hag confronted and accused him. Just then a flock of geese flew overhead. One of them was wounded. Three drops of its blood fell onto the soft white snow. And Parsifal was transfixed.

This spellbound state symbolises the call of the soul, when the Chakra wheels will begin the turn the other way. The mystery of the blood awakens Parsifal from unconscious slumber. And he must find that thing which has spiritual value and meaning within him and with which he will serve the greater good. As yet, however, he is still lost, limited and unaware of his true spiritual destiny.

As the Chakra wheels turn, they draw up those psychological bloodline issues. These are our psychic inheritance. Distant cries from the deep, dark within are the cries of our fathers and their fathers before them calling us to release them from the seven Chakra wheels upon which they are bound fast as with chains. The Chakras turn as yet the opposite way to freedom. That way, however, was directed by those lives that went before us. It is the way of selfishness and of suffering. It is the downward spiral into the dark.

When this happens, the individual may begin to relive experiences that are deeply disturbing—out of proportion with anything related to the individual's personal life. The individual has touched the deeper psychic thoughtforms—remnants of the past—unresolved ancestral longings.

Lives that are traumatised or unfulfilled continue to flow in the bloodline awaiting the time when the blood shall be healed.

The idea of waiting for the saviour to come is ancient and common to all cultures. It is the task of the bloodline to create a Parsifal—the one who has the power of mind and heart to enter the mists and journey into the darkness of the underworld in order to turn the Chakra wheels the other way. S/he will free her or his ancestors by atoning for their sins.

This sounds like Karma or Original Sin. However, insight given me by *Amrita* differs from commonly understood interpretations. We are not communing with a personal Karma—rather an inherited Karma. It is this we must heal.

My inspiration on the Grail myth and Joseph's message reveals the importance of recognising that our ancestors *live* in our blood. We are living out their patterns of incarnation. Perhaps some of these experiences that are thought to be from past lives are actually ancient memories, or *thoughtforms,* passed on by our ancestral bloodline.

The esoteric teachings tell us that *the blood is the seat of the soul.* The ancestral or group soul is incarnate through the bloodline. As personalities we die. But the life of the soul is eternal. And the soul continues to seek incarnation until the bloodline produces its own saviour—a Christ of her or his own time.

Flowing into the nadis, sentient energy from the *astral world* makes its way into physical expression.

The astral world is the watery feeling realm of illusion. In this world, good and bad freely intermingle and are lost in a sea of emotional reaction. It is the world under-mind—the natural world of the child, as the child lives predominantly in its *astral body.* This world coexists in time and space with our physical world. Moving through matter, wraithlike and alien, strange and disturbing, it engenders in all of us the fear of that which is unknown.

Out of the collective pool of astral energy, each astral body is created. Made out of substance from all levels of man's emotional existence, this body enables us to experience the full range of planetary sentient life— from divine realms of spiritual aspiration, to worlds of gross desire.

The astral body is the keeper of experiences of the feeling world. Worn down by emotional living, the astral body is permanently dying. It must struggle constantly to recreate itself. Drawing from its surrounding emotional environment the astral matter necessary to fulfil its task, it attracts to itself substance of similar kind.

This is how *Synchronicity* works.

Our astral bodies become what they psychically absorb. To substance of like kind, searching tentacles turn, to feel their way into familiar energy. Thus, though we grow old, in essence we remain emotionally the same, feeding and suckling the same nectar and the same poison from outer experiences. Thus does our astral body constantly rebuild itself in the same pattern as the old.

Changing the vibration of the astral body is essential in the initiation process. This is the only way we transform the negative ancestral bloodline issues. Astral bodies derive energy from the same dense substance that feeds collective fear, insecurity, guilt, ignorance and self-pity. The astral body then remains so tightly knit that the forces of light that rule the evolution of consciousness cannot penetrate.

Crying is nature's inner cleansing process. And in one whose tears have flushed clean the lurking shadows and cried them into the light of day, the astral body becomes a more efficient vehicle capable of conscious feeling and independent action. It has learned to discriminate between the world of emotional reaction and the yet deeper feeling world of soul.

Deep beneath the astral body's watery surface is the true world of soul-feeling. It is the pure world of love, compassion, and paradoxically, the source of our painful psychological issues.

The soul is the prisoner of the form, locked within a body that never knows it. Expressing itself through form, the soul feels the loss of its own world. Misunderstood by the physical world of humankind, its truths are alien to the physical pull of our natural desire nature. Lack of recognition, sense of loss, abandonment, rejection, aloneness, despair at not being able to express itself are the feelings of the soul that are unbearable for us to experience.

Although exquisite in their depth, they are too painful. If felt, they send us plummeting into despair and set us apart from a purely physical world that does not want to experience its own pain. If it did, it would realise that in experiencing pain, transformation is possible. We would awaken our hearts. Our Chakra wheels would turn the other way. We would enter into the purgatory of all souls and set free our ancestors from thought-forms that repeat *our* suffering.

Distorted as it filters its way through the upper layers of the emotional world, the pain of soul is swallowed up in emotional reaction. We project our issues of injustice, unfairness, abandonment, need, rejection and self-pity onto the world. We distort the pain of the soul into anger against each other. We expect others to fill the deep and aching void within each of us. And when others cannot, we are continuously disappointed and always seeking some outside distraction to make the pain disappear.

Sometimes in the depths of an individual's astral body, I see a constantly changing turbulence, whilst the surface of it remains glassy smooth. The surface of the astral body is frozen, suspended in an unconscious state of shock, leaving powerful emotional undercurrents no outlet for expression. Sentient life is blocked.

This is trauma—a dangerous state of being—leading to somatic symptoms, organ tissue damage, depression or disease.

But the feelings of the soul registered in the astral body are archetypal feelings impossible to be rid of. Original and inherent, they are the deepest feelings common to all. To have them is to have soul—and that is the task of humanity.

As I travel still deeper into the subtle worlds, I see in them energy raised in vibration onto new levels of existence. Each body is finer than the last and each is more beautiful.

The *mental body* appears as a tongue of flame licking its way through space. Turning in a circle, the hungry fire flicks out to pull from the midnight blue of space communications from higher worlds.

This is the ovoid space separating the mental world from the world of physical mind. This space is the true vehicle of the soul and is the passive receiver of direct spirit knowledge.

In this deep, silent space, stillness waits.

A message from the spirit world is seized—devoured by the hungry fire of mind, digested, translated, then birthed. Exploding into myriads of sparkling Colours then cascading like waterfalls that have been dazzled by the sun, the Colours fall like fiery rain upon the astral body where they are reflected in the deep. Mixed then with emotional response, they travel on—carried in rivulets through the nadis—to be redirected onwards by the Chakras, eventually entering the etheric substance that interpenetrates and builds the physical brain.

The spirit has spoken the language of Colour, which is the language of the gods. The mental body has translated it into the language of the soul, which is the universal language of symbolism. Whilst the physical brain has interpreted its meaning according to the framework of knowledge at its disposal. The brain sends its signals through the nervous system, which manifests eventually as physical response.

All energy is an expression of life. All energy is sacred. All the different bodies are vehicles of the spirit. As in the notes of the scale, the root note is repeated in the octave. Although these notes are the same, they are raised to higher vibrations. It is the same with the bodies. They vibrate at different speeds, creating different hues. As the speed of their vibration increases, they become more finely tuned and are more responsive to subtler energy waves. Our different vehicles of expression give us the opportunity to respond to the full range of stimuli—ranging from physical to spiritual vibrations—that we may express all we are. Each vehicle sounds its own note, has its own vibratory hue and expresses its own coexistent identity.

The mental body is the most sensitive of all our feeling equipment. Good thoughts produce responsive vibrations in the finer matter in the body and tell the endocrine glands to secrete their elixirs into the bloodstream. These elixirs are positive hormones, considered by the ancients to be the *Elixir of Life*. Negative thoughts, such as denied anger produce poisons, which are also secreted by the glands into the bloodstream.

As a wo-man thinks, so is s/he.

Each one of us most constantly affects the condition of our own health, that of each other's, and that of the environment's.

*T*he occult healer who has passed through spiritual initiation knows how to build a thought until it becomes a *form*.

The thought is imbued with will. It is created from intention. Clothed then in etheric, astral and mental energy so that it may perform its particular task, it is directed to the afflicted part of the body. Travelling along the etheric web, it moves into the etheric body of the person for whom it is intended. There, it completes its work.

Thoughts become for a time living creatures capable of intense activity. These fiery little salamanders are commanded by the healer to reveal, breakdown, re-educate and transform old thoughtforms that have been trapped in the body and are the creators of the disease.

Thoughts are also the builders of tissue. They rebuild it by gathering about the affected part energy of similar vibration.

*A*nd this is how the ancient masters of the wisdom created the Glastonbury Zodiac. They created *Thoughtforms,* capable of independent life. They knew how to clothe them and make them live. Out of etheric, astral and mental energy, they created the zodiac around which the land would eventually take shape.

Eighteen

Entrance to the Underworld

The name, Parsifal, means pierce-the-veil. *Amrita* bids the Parsifals amongst us to enter the mists that veil the underworld…

Only the descent into the darkness of unconsciousness
can release you from ancestral thoughtforms
that keep you in bondage.
Then must you descend into the greater darkness,
into the purgatory of all souls
and atone for them,
who descended into darkness,
with their lives unresolved.

Free your ancestors from their suffering,
those abandoned souls,
crying out for recognition and for redemption.

Your destiny is to heal the bloodline.

You, the Parsifals of your own time,
must find the chalice.
Open your hearts and purify them.
Confront the demons that lurk in the shadows.
Know yourselves.

This is the way to unity with each other.

Awaken the compassionate man
who sleeps at the heart of the feminine world,
the direct descendant of Christ.

This is the power of the chalice.

The chalice is within.
The chalice contains the blood of Christ.

The bloodline of Christ shall heal the world.

Amrita summons all seekers to the portal of initiation—to the Avalon of their own beings. This mystical entrance is to be found at the back of the head. This is the centre in the body known as the *alta major.*

The alta major is the chakra that governs the *carotid gland.* Not considered to be one of the major seven, its value is often overlooked—its secrets locked away. *Amrita* revealed to me that it is the *back door* to the unconscious—the secret entrance to the inner world.

Psychic remnants of ancient civilisations, past deeds of ancestors, legend-makers filled with the power of kings—all of whom shaped our world, are buried behind its locked doors. The secrets of our past await the time when we shall be ready to know them.

The alta major is the *inner tree of life.* It is the tree upon which we are crucified—upon which the personal will is sacrificed to the greater *Will of Spirit.*

The spine is the trunk of the alta major tree. It burrows deep into the base chakra, where the root of the spine draws energy from the mother earth. She feeds us with the will-to-survive. For she is the giver and preserver of life.

The branches of the alta major tree reach up to the heavens within us, to the crown centre—seat of the *Spiritual Will.* Governed by the *pineal gland*, the crown centre is also known as the *Thousand Petalled Lotus.* Upon this throne, the energy of the father principle reigns supreme. He stimulates us with the will-to-evolve and is the giver of the purpose of life.

Throughout the ages, the alta major has controlled our physical and emotional development, blending Heaven's purpose with forms created of earth. *Amrita* revealed how, thousands of years ago, spiritual man began to emerge.

The pineal gland, influenced by Heaven's Will, greatly stimulated the development of the *pituitary gland*. The pituitary gland is the governing gland of the *endocrine system* and directly affects our health—for good or ill. Called by some the third eye, the pituitary gland governs the *ajna centre* which is the chakra situated in the middle of the forehead. It is the future, forward looking, and the seat of the Self, where the energy of spiritual will meets the energy of the personality. Together, these blended energies create a *Self* worthy to be ruler of the inner kingdom.

The newly developing pituitary gland influenced the development of the carotid gland. In response to incoming *Will of Universal Spirit*, the pituitary gland bade the carotid gland to straighten man's spine. And reaching for the destiny that was written in the stars, man stood tall for the first time and left his four legged brothers behind forever.

The old brain, still ruled by the alta major, is the part of ourselves that is instinctual. Situated at the back of the head, it symbolises that which we've forgotten—our past and our roots. When survival is threatened, and in the case of the human being this means emotional survival also, the alta major sends urgent signals to the base chakra. The will-to-survive is then energised, commanding the adrenal glands to secrete adrenaline into the blood stream. This extra help gives us the power to fight, or run.

Our system has been fed with the elixir of survival enabling us to stay in control and keep our senses clear and sharp until all threat of danger, whether physical or emotional, has passed. Paradoxically, the alta major makes us stay in control of our emotions. As long as we hold on to that control, the healing process can never begin. The door to the psyche remains locked.

The closed alta major is like the iron fist of will clenched in defiance of the self. It holds back emotion, keeping our feelings trapped in our bodies, thus also preventing our chakras from opening and releasing not only pain, but also, potential.

Learning the *right* use of the will is the secret that will open the heart.

Often people pride themselves on their strong wills. Feelings are never allowed to show. Vulnerability is considered weakness. The alta major is tightly shut. Chains of pride and duty bind them. They misuse the will against the self.

If the alta major tree stands tall and rigid, unmoved by the winds of change, it must eventually snap, broken by the storm, instead of being shaped by it.

Spiritual growth demands that we open our chakras into full service and life, swinging all that we are into the light—including ancestral horrors. Our ancestors are in our blood. The blood is the seat of the soul. Thus every life ever lived by them is forever held within the soul's knowledge. It is the soul's task to resolve the pain of our ancestral bloodline in order that we gain our true inheritance—the positive power of our roots. This is the energy that will feed our crown, and make us wise rulers of the kingdom within.

Now at the turn of the age, the lord of the underworld demands transformation. He demands that we lay our ancestors to rest. Their unresolved thoughtforms have been the structures upon which our unconscious lives are lived. These structures must be allowed to crumble, their rancid decay transformed into the compost that will feed and strengthen the spirit for new undertakings. If we do not heed this lord when he calls for transformation, we begin to die the slow and painful death of rigid resistance to change.

Nineteen

Dark Night of the Soul

e would never choose to enter the underworld, never willingly, unless called to the task by the god of transformation. He is the god who presides over initiation and death.

He wills that we face the night and walk for a time in his world of shadows.

This is the world of the collective unconscious—the dark and deep so natural to fear. Ruled over by our collective denials, it is a world only visited in nightmares, when a bitter sleep is the bringer of a loss of conscious control.

If we go there, loneliness and despair will be constant companions. They will claw at our hearts and pull out our insides. They will feed our entrails to the crows. We will be as Promethean figures suffering the torment inflicted by outraged ego gods of selfishness and spite.

We will attest how isolated we are. We will attest how loneliness feeds despair.

This is the monster we wrestle with in order to keep him at bay. By distracting ourselves away from the power of his gaze, we succeeded in shutting him behind the heavy door of unconsciousness. We even managed to bolt it fast, thinking that we had permanently locked the monster inside. But all the while, the monster grew, its power dammed up behind the strong door that held it back. And as its power grew it was able to summon the army of vices that live in deep dark underground burrows.

Vices make a lethal army. They are acts of a hardened and embittered heart that holds on to emotional pain. Small enough, they slip unnoticed beneath the heavy door of unconsciousness. They attack us with their poison. It freezes our hearts and seeps into our minds, and makes us perfect instruments of attack upon our fellow men.

89

At the helm of the army of vices, self-justification rides his chariot. With his talent, he is able to exonerate us from any personal blame.

Throughout our lives, the pain we lock away in dark and dreary inner dungeons can only turn inwards and feed off the deeper, more ancient pain of our ancestors. As a result, it grows fat and hard like an emotional cancer eroding love. And it makes us continue to commit the sin of Cain against Abel because we shut our hearts to our fellow men. For whether we raise our hand against another or not, our unnoticed vices have the power to destroy.

Vices are feelings that are so totally unlovable, they are forced to live underground like rats in hiding. Their most potent weapon against our recognition of them is their subtlety. If we could identify them easily, they would lose their power over us. But unfortunately, they are so much a part of us all as to be totally unnoticeable. We simply cannot see their coldness. Instead, we prefer to send their poisonous darts into the feeling bodies of others, subtly eroding their self-esteem and adding to an ocean of collective hatred.

Thus we are all responsible for creating and supporting the never-ending burden of emotional pain commonly shared by us all.

Book Four
Symbols of Transformation

Twenty

Parsifal's Tale

Whilst some myths are metaphors attempting to express the ubiquitous presence that underlies creation itself, others weave tales of the unconscious and encapsulate our *spiritual DNA*.

Paradoxically, the word myth is often taken to mean a lie or abstraction, something unreal or imagined—almost a superstitious belief. Many cultures, however, express their spirituality through myth. Myths speak a language that transcends all barriers of race and creed. Myths are allegories of the *inner* life—parables retelling the dramatic journey of the soul.

The Parsifal story is one such myth. It takes us across the great divide—from conscious reality into the realms of shadow, soul and spirit. It is a tale of the collective unconscious.

I had been living the Parsifal myth. Synchronistically this inner theatre had been reflected in physical externalised events—in *profound coincidences*. The reality of the myth overwhelmed my personal life. I was living a life determined by a collective need.

On the surface of it, Parsifal's adventures appear as a simple story, a myth within a myth—part of the Arthurian sagas and legends of the Holy Grail. It is the kind of story we tell our children to foster in them the concept of spiritual quest and sacred mystery.

Parsifal was the son of Alain Li Gros, who was grandson to *Joseph of Arimathea.*

Parsifal, however, did not know his father. He had been a great knight who had been killed in battle fighting the holy wars for Richard the

93

Lionheart. Parsifal's brothers had also died in battle alongside their father.

Parsifal's mother did not want her only remaining son to meet the same fate, so she had taken him to live with her in the forest to keep him from the world of knights, damsels, arms and heroic deeds.

Thus Parsifal grew up overprotected by his mother, and innocent of the power of the bloodline pulsing through his veins. Relentlessly, it drove him to the rhythm of an ancient drum and was the quickening beat of heart that compelled him to follow.

One day, whilst out collecting wood in the forest, Parsifal saw two knights hunting. So brightly shone their armour that he thought he was in the presence of angels. One time, as a very little boy, he had asked his mother what angels looked like. She had told him they shone like the sun. Parsifal, being so young and naive, always took everything his mother had said literally. And as his eyes were nearly blinded by what he now saw before him, he fell to his knees and cried out to the knights to stop and tell him what made them shine so.

The knights gazed on the boy's countenance turned in awed supplication towards them. And seeing the innocence there, they decided not to kill him. Perhaps he would be sport instead. So they told him of Arthur, the king, and how it was he who had given them their shining armour.

Arthur was the greatest king in all the land.

To Parsifal, this meant Arthur was God. How could it be otherwise when his mother had told him that God made the angels? Parsifal had never seen anything so beautiful. So he made a resolution deep within his heart and soul to become a knight—one of God's angels here on earth.

No matter what she does, thought Parsifal on his way home, I shall be a glorious knight. My mother shall not stop me. She is not brave and strong like those shining men. In the morning I will tell her that I am leaving to seek out Arthur.

When Parsifal told his mother his news, she fainted. And in that moment, he broke free of her power.

Parsifal would work his own will.

His mother eventually realised that she had to let him go. She saw the fire burning in his eyes. And silently, she cursed the fate that had been so strong as to wrench him from her. She would still do her best though, to keep him from harm. It may be the last thing she could ever do for him.

She made him a cloth tunic, such as those worn by the welsh peasantry, and gave him an old nag to be his trusty steed. This old beast could never fly with him into battle. And his welsh tunic was no armour to lead anyone to believe that this was a fighting man. He would pass for a fool. Arthur would think him so. As would all the rest. They would all laugh. And when no one would take him seriously, then would he realise his foolishness and return to her, his loving mother.

But she hadn't bargained for the power of the unknown father who lived on in Parsifal's blood inciting in him the inner spiritual violence necessary for one who is to be a true seeker. He would abandon her and break her heart.

That morning as he rode away, his mother's parting words floated behind him on the very lightest of breezes. "Honour women," she cried, "Pray in every church you shall find, and take the ring of a woman if she should so offer it." His mother's words were already an echo. Without a backward glance, Parsifal began his journey, away from his mother, away from his home, and forward to freedom, Camelot, and King Arthur.

Very soon, Parsifal came to a tent. He could not help his curiosity, which was insatiable. So he drew aside the tent flap and went inside. A beautiful woman lay asleep.

Lured by some overwhelming magic of hers, he had crossed the tent in seconds. Her softness held his gaze. Strangely stirred, he put his lips on top of hers. That was, however, all he had time for. Suddenly, the softly breathing, shimmering loveliness awoke, spitting.

She stared at him, at first afraid. But then, as she became aware of the very beautiful boy who stood above her with his mouth gaping open in wonder, she sat up. "What are you doing in here?" she asked.

"My husband will return soon and slice you into strips of hide and hang you out to dry!"

Parsifal could say nothing. He couldn't hear her words, just the rich timbre in the voice that spoke them. And she began to wonder if, in fact, he didn't look a bit simple. Maybe she should use sign language. Perhaps he was deaf. So she took off her ring. "Look!" she cried, holding out the ring for him to see, "I am a married woman. Didn't you hear me?"

And with that, Parsifal snatched the ring he thought she'd proffered him, and made off into the night, confused and dissatisfied.

When her husband, the duke, returned that night to his wife, he sensed that things were not as they had been when he left. His eyes were alerted to the large set of footprints in the sand, and they led straight to his wife's bed.

Now the Duke L'Orguelleus de la Lande had never been known as a reasonable man. His method was to act first and ask questions later. Immediately consumed by jealousy and convinced of his wife's infidelity, he screamed his madness so that it shook the night. Then he battered her with his fists. He would have eventually left it at that if he had not then discovered that her ring was not on her finger. Now all his fears were confirmed. Beating was too good for her. He would have to think of something else.

It wasn't long before his rage came up with an idea: a fitting punishment to suit her crime. He would not listen to her sweet reassurances, or to her pleas of innocence. So he tied her naked, sitting backwards on an ass, and made her ride through rain and cold, and night and weary day, shamed and dishonoured. He would make her ride the length and breadth of the land until her lover found her. And then he could kill them both.

Meanwhile, Parsifal rode on to Camelot, oblivious. And as he approached the great moat, it seemed as if a huge red flame burst past him. The flame slowed, and Parsifal could see that it was in fact the brilliant red of the armour worn by a huge and ferocious knight.

"Boy!" bellowed the brilliant red knight. "Do my will! Tell Arthur, he shall not have his golden cup back until he comes for it himself."

And then the red knight, who was most feared by all, rode off, bawling for his own amusement.

Parsifal sat on his old nag, wondering.

And this is how Parsifal was said to come into the presence of the great king, who must be God. He stood before him, before all the fine court of ladies and knights who were snickering to themselves. He wore no shoes. His hair was tousled. His appearance was unkempt. And he was clothed only in the hairy tunic of Welsh peasantry. He was obviously a fool.

"A pity!" thought one of the women. "He is a beautiful fool."

He had strutted in to deliver the message from the red knight, and had pronounced to all the court that he had come to be made to shine like the angels.

The king was not amused. The red knight had defiantly stolen one of the golden goblets and spilled its contents over his lady Guinevere, queen of all of Britain. He had then rode out in triumph knocking down three of his best men-in-arms hewing and hacking his way through their flesh and bone. Then, to add insult to injury, he had sent this simpleton as his emissary to deliver an even bloodier challenge.

The simpleton was, however, still in front of him, fervently declaring to all the court that he would fight the red knight and save His Majesty's honour by retrieving, single-handed, the cup. And while he was at it, he would also relieve the red knight of his armour and his horse.

Arthur's court was beginning to erupt into open hilarity. It wasn't worth stringing up this foolish little upstart who called himself Parsifal. The red knight would save them all the bother. "Go then!" shouted Arthur. "And if you succeed, then shall I make you a knight."

The court cheered and clapped and laughed, and Parsifal thought they were laughing because he had pleased them.

Full of the sounds of their merriment in his ears, Parsifal rode out to his first battle. Greed for the armour of the red knight spurred him on. He was within hours of achieving his greatest dream. Surely his mother would be proud of him. But he didn't want to think of her. She was

97

weak, and it made him feel bad to think of her. His eyes shut their memory of her away in some other place. He was riding out to meet his fate. Silently, he avowed to himself, fearless and ruthlessly determined, that before the sun had set on this day, he would be a knight.

It wasn't long before Parsifal found the red knight sitting lazily beneath a large spreading oak. "King sent his scullery boy to ask me to be polite and give him back his pretty cup?" jeered the huge red man. "Look! Why here it is! It's in my hand." The knight's eyes glinted with evil, as Parsifal noticed that a sword was in his other hand.

"Then I'll just have to take it from you," replied the youth. And with that, Parsifal leapt forward and with one blow of the sword he had stolen on his way out of the castle, he severed the knight's weaponed arm. "It was much like chopping wood," thought Parsifal of his first killing blow, as he moved in to finish the job.

The knight had been taken totally by surprise. He hadn't expected this fool to attack him. He roared his agony and tried to leap to his feet, but it was much too late for him. And wrestling with death that was fast upon him, he registered his one last thought. "Of all men, I, the great red knight, who has slaughtered and plundered and sent fear throughout all the land, have finally been defeated by a fool." And on that, his very last realisation, he died.

Parsifal was triumphant. He had his armour. Just some blood to clean off and it would be as good as new and brightly shining as ever. It was very difficult, though, to get the body of the knight out the armour. But, as the story goes, Parsifal, ingenious as ever, decided to boil it out. Thus, Parsifal, the fool, claimed his armour and put it on over the welsh tunic his mother had given him. And upon his newly acquired horse, he rode back to Camelot to return the stolen goblet to Arthur, much to everyone's amazement and not least, to the king's.

Thus did Parsifal the fool, become a knight, and become known, in turn, as the Red Knight.

There was a man at Arthur's court—a great teacher of arms and knightly etiquette, named Gornemant de Goort. He decided to train this young lad in the skills of weaponry and chivalry. He thought Parsifal had shown so much bravado, fearlessness and natural talent that he could see in him the makings of a great knight, even if there were still the scoffers who thought the red knight's death had been but a lucky fluke.

Gornemant, however, saw something else in Parsifal: a deep and burning intensity rare in one so young. He would help this young man to develop his talent.

And so the training had begun. Day and night, he worked Parsifal, testing the boy's mettle, urging him on to new challenges and watching him with pride. Daily, Parsifal impressed. No task was too great, no challenge turned away from. Secretly, Gornemant suspected that this boy would be the greatest of all his pupils.

There was, however, one very annoying trait of the boy's: his insatiable curiosity. He was always asking stupid questions about things that everyone knew the answers to. He must break the boy of the habit, or he would always appear the fool. A knight must inspire confidence. He must always appear to be all-knowing and strong.

It was this instruction that would, however, eventually lead to Parsifal's downfall.

Eventually, came the time for Parsifal to set out into the world in search of knightly deeds. At the back of his mind was the desire to find his way back to his mother's house to make her proud of him. With this intention, he went on his way, leaving Camelot, Gornemant, and Arthur behind.

His path led him to a castle that was besieged. With fire in his belly and a thirst for more killing, Parsifal set his horse's head towards his next knightly deed. And he was not disappointed. For this was the home of Blanchflor, a maiden of great beauty whom none could rival.

Cruelly, had her castle been under attack for many weeks now. And there were only weaklings to protect her when eventually the siege broke and her castle must open its gates. Otherwise, all its inhabitants would die of starvation.

She didn't care. She would die sooner than give herself to those who had made her a prisoner in her own home.

A few barbarians, however, were no match for Parsifal. His newly acquired skills, added to his unsullied passion for battle soon made light work of Blanchflor's foes.

Who was this mistress he was hearing so much of? His mind flashed back to the other creature that had left him aching for something he didn't understand. Would she be another one like that? The thought of that quickened his pace. And as the last head rolled, surprised, onto the grass, Parsifal called out to be permitted to enter—with his lady's permission, of course! Gornemant had taught him well.

And so Blanchflor became the lady of a knight, bonded to him as her rescuer. And such a beautiful knight was he. A bright, shining and hungry young man. She would teach him love. It wouldn't be difficult. Not the way his eyes devoured her every time he saw her. As hers did him. Both of them virgins, she could tell. But soon, very soon, not to be. What fate had brought him to her—her match at last? And he learned so fast. She had only to tell him something once, and it was forever his—his, to please her with. Glorious love! Saved from the vicious arms of death, by the strong gentle arms of such a virile and young saviour!

She would hold him forever under the spell cast by her beauty. And she would make him wait—just long enough.

And Parsifal had found his woman. He was now a lady's knight, and had accomplished his first task. All knights must serve a lady, and this lady was beautiful. Somehow, though, she always eluded him. In some strange way, she had power. She reminded him of his mother. And that made him want to know, conquer and possess her.

Thus, Parsifal learned the art of love and the magic of being in love. His flame grew bright. And he gave her all, until he felt another urge beginning to eat away at him. It was the call to more deeds. New conquests began to beckon. He began to feel claustrophobic. Again, he remembered his mother. Again, he would go out in search of her and bring her to live with Blanchflor. They could keep each other company. And he would be free to pursue other things. To have both women in his life under one roof was an idea full of appeal. Parsifal had now learned enough about women to realise that they would keep an eye on each other.

Again he rode out. And again, he came to a different castle to the one he sought—the likes of which he had never seen before. Strange things took place there before his eyes—none of which he understood and none of which he questioned.

A king who was the keeper of something called the Grail; another, much older king who was ailing and suffering; a maiden who carried a chalice filled with blood—a bleeding lance, a broken sword—passed in front of him in procession in a court in which he was being sumptuously feasted. But, Parsifal, remembering Gornemant's words, did not question. He felt too drunk on the ambience of the scene—as though wrapped in a dream. So Parsifal ate the food, drank the wine and fell asleep.

When he awoke, he was in a very comfortable bed, yet couldn't remember how he got there. He called out, but no one answered. He got up to look, but the castle was empty. So he left, shaking the hangover out of his head.

As soon as he had crossed the drawbridge it shut fast and firm behind him. But he hadn't seen the hand that had drawn it. Nor had he seen the hand that made the castle disappear before his very eyes. " Whatever that wine had been, it must have been good!" thought he.

Slowly, his ears awoke to the sound of sobbing nearby. "Oh well!" he decided, "Another damsel in distress. No time to stand here blinking my eyes all day! Better get on with the business of being a knight."

She was sitting by a lake, rocking to and fro, nursing the headless body of a knight in her arms. The dismembered head of the knight was placed on the bank. It stared blindly back at her.

She looked up as Parsifal approached. Her eyes narrowed to a sting. "I am related to you," she told him. "I am here to tell you that your mother died of grief when you left her. You failed your test in the Grail castle just now. You failed to heal the Wounded Fisher King! Now healing shall not be brought to the land, and everything shall remain barren and suffering as before." And with that, she carried on rocking and sobbing and nursing her knight in her lap.

Just then, a flock of wild geese flew by overhead. A falcon was chasing them. One of the geese was wounded. Three drops of its blood fell onto the crisp snow that had been falling since morning. Red on white. Suddenly, Parsifal was transfixed, lost in a reverie, held to the sight of red blood falling on white snow.

The most grotesque of hags one could ever imagine was standing before him, pointing a long sinewy finger straight at his heart.

Parsifal was beginning to lose a grip on things. He wanted to get as far away as possible from this place and this new apparition. Damsels in distress were one thing, but this aberration of femininity, was quite another. And he wasn't in the mood for whatever this old witch might spring on him. He needed time to digest everything, especially the news about his mother.

But, he could not move. The spell cast by the drops of blood in the snow still held him and gave the hag strange powers over him. Ominous and loathsome, she continued to point her long filthy index finger in accusation.

Twenty One

The Question is the Key

*Myths are timeless, placeless,
needing only the right question
to be asked of the self.*

*The self knows past, present and future.
The right question asked of the self
is the key to the door
that opens unto the world of mysteries.*

amrita

The **Holy Grail** symbolises the thing that has spiritual value and meaning. It is found only by inward searching into unconscious realms, and questioning all we witness there.

Parsifal is a fool because he does not question. He takes things literally.

One of the symbols in the myth depicts a weeping girl nursing the headless body of a knight. Her tears accuse Parsifal of his failure. He had not questioned the meaning of the mysterious procession, nor the ailing and wounded king whose agony was apparent. Instead, he had got drunk on the wine and had fallen asleep. He had missed his opportunity to achieve something of real meaning and value. He had thus relegated his destiny back to the shadow realm of unconsciousness.

If we do not question the meaning of a dream, illness or synchronistic event, we are missing an opportunity for communion with the soul.

We also ignore our doubts. Doubts are really questions. They are rites of passage. Parsifal had been trained that a good knight does not ask questions. Paradoxically, in fulfilling his conditioning and carrying out what was expected of him, he had committed a crime against his soul.

Feeling, meaning questions are the keys that unlock the door of the psyche. These are not quantitative, but qualitative questions—not rational, but non-rational: "How do I *feel* about that?" "What does this *mean* to me?" "*Why* am I doubting this?"

When these questions are asked of the Self in the spirit of heartfelt inquiry, chakras open and spill out their contents. Ancient issues that cause not only personal suffering, but also racial suffering, are raised into the light of consciousness.

These issues are expressed in representational images. When questioned yet more deeply, they will transform us.

Twenty Two

Symbols of Transformation

The soul speaks in symbols.
Its quiet call out of the darkness needs to be heard.
But it can only be heard with our hearts.

The heart translates the language of symbols.
The heart feels their meaning.
If the language of symbols is not heard with the heart,
the images expressed by the soul
remain as lifeless things.
Their power to transform us is lost.
And the soul's life passes unnoticed,
back into the world of shadows.

amrita

The Hag is a symbol of our inner ugliness.

She comes to inculpate us of our own inner disfigurement. All the feelings we disown turn into the blistering sores that disfigure her face. She is carrier of our burden of unexpressed emotion. Her back is crooked beneath its weight.

Most of us do not want to admit how inwardly ugly our thoughts and perverted emotions make us. When the Hag comes to accuse us, she makes us aware of the ugliness of these forces that hold sway over waking consciousness. We are ready to face our denials—to stop blaming others for our hurts. We are ready to own and recognise *the psychological matrix* that keeps our emotional life twisted and ugly.

This psychological matrix is collective. We are all conceived of it. It is a transpersonally inherited, *misuse of masculine and feminine energies*. *Masculine and feminine* are metaphors. They are *principles*—universal laws—not limited to gender. They describe *Yin and Yang*, earth and heaven, soul and spirit. They are expressed in the contra-sexual *anima and animus* in each of us.

The feminine principle is the *Receptive*. It is water, soul, being, caring and feeling. It is that which gives meaning and value to things. The masculine principle is the *Creative*. It is the urge to action. It is fire, spirit and drive. It is desire, the law of force, power, will and purpose. We distort both these principles and make them ugly through our mis-handling of them. Then we play them out in our relationships with each other.

One of the motifs in the Parsifal story depicts *a flock of geese* that flies overhead pursued by a falcon. One of the geese is wounded. Three drops of its blood fall onto the soft white snow—red on white—symbol of Yang and Yin—symbol of inner unity. The goose represents Blanch-flor. The bird who preys on her is Parsifal. The Hag accuses Parsifal of failing to achieve inner unity. He has wounded his own feminine principle.

We wound our feminine principle by not listening to our feelings. We do not trust them. We rationalise or deny them completely. Our femi-nine principle is treated as if it were a silly goose. It is controlled, domi-nated and disrespected. We commit this inner crime through the *misuse of the will* against the self.

Vulnerability is a truth. It is seen as weakness. The feminine principle is not ambitious. It is therefore seen as serving no useful purpose. The feminine principle measures life by how it feels and how others feel. It experiences rather than analyses. It is the inner nurturer and would nourish us if we allowed it.

So often feeling is made analogous with emotion. Feeling is not the same as emotion. Feeling is the *function* by which we *feel* the emotion.

A function works for us. Different functions work in different ways. The thinking function is metaphorically masculine. It orders and sifts information, past and present, and in this way comes to a rational conclu-sion based on concrete information. The feeling function is metaphori-cally feminine. According to Carl Jung, it is the other rational function alongside thinking. It is not the emotion—but stands outside of it. It is not swallowed up by it. At the same time it is able to feel the emotion because it is of like kind.

The feeling function is the organ of perception by which we are able to *consciously identify*, relate, and give value to our experiences and emotions. If well developed, it is able to penetrate emotion and grasp its underlying matrix.

This is a rational process of entering into the non-rational inner realms. For example: "I feel angry"! Anger is the emotion. *I feel*, is an act of identification—an act of conscious recognition by which we have a relationship with the emotion. "What do I feel angry about?" This is the next question asked by the feeling function that seeks to penetrate the emotion. When the answer comes, it will be something like... "I'm feeling emotional because that person was unfair to me..."

Feeling penetrates feelings. If feeling, meaning, questions are asked of the self, the feeling function *sees* deeper into the personal pain of old issues—such as unfairness. In this way, the feeling consciousness of the individual is able to realise that the person who was unfair is the trigger but not the cause.

The cause originates in a deep-seated, unvalued feeling that has become charged with emotion. The feeling has become an issue. It may originate from a childhood event. But the scale of the emotional reaction is determined by our own inborn, innate, *predispositions*.

Emotions are the keys to our personal issues.

When we ask the right questions of our emotions, they will lead us deep into the psyche. Eventually we realise how we are accessories in the act of unfairness. We recognise our own unseen urge—the abysmal predisposition towards being profoundly unfair to ourselves.

These issues are paradoxical. Whilst on the one hand they are blind emotional responses that drive us unconsciously, often with the proverbial chip on our shoulder; on the other hand, they are triggers for the thing we most deeply care about.

Emotional reactions are *distorted responses of the soul.*

When we manage to untangle our complexes by working with them consciously, we feel how we may begin to serve our soul's purpose. The lifelong cross we have borne is transformed into our greatest gift. We find our true work in the world and live the purpose for which we were born.

A deep sense of injustice creates fighters for justice. A sense of being unloved creates humanitarian practitioners. A sense of lack of recognition creates a person who readily gives recognition to others. An issue with abandonment creates a soul who never abandons others. A traumatic childhood creates an adult who positively re-parents the child in many.

Most of us have to learn to recognise what we are feeling. Emotions are so often allowed to spill out in such inappropriate ways that cause damage to others, whether psychically through acts of an aggressive mind, or through acts of physical violence.

Culturally, we do not respect or understand the purpose of emotional reaction. We live in a society that suppresses emotions, disrespects feelings, and does not value personal experience. It judges, rationalises, misunderstands and distorts them. Emotions not listened to fester into something unwholesome. They become issues, complexes and neuroses. They are made ugly and cause sickness both personal and societal.

When the Hag comes to accuse us, she shows us that the cause of our suffering lies within ourselves. It lies in our ignorance of the unconscious that holds such powerful sway over waking reality. When we realise this, we can no longer take refuge in blaming others.

We are *all* co-creators of the abuse of the feminine world.

The Hag is the embodiment of a collective thoughtform created by humanity because of centuries of denial of the feminine principle. She is a feminine embodiment of conscience—a messenger of the soul.

Deep within us, the Hag now demands recognition. She, being one of the expressions of our feminine nature, is an expression of the soul made ugly. She has been willing to carry the heavy burden of our denials. We have imposed on her too long. It is time for us to release her from the prison of ugliness to which she has been condemned.

Feelings need to be acknowledged. When they are, they are transformed back into something positive and light bearing. This is the message of the Hag. Through conscious recognition of our own inner ugliness, the Hag will be transformed into her original shape. She will be made beautiful again.

We see this motif expressed in fairy tales: the princess (the finer feeling nature) is often turned into a goose by the wicked witch. It is the task of the handsome young prince (the noble spirit) to save her from her cruel fate. His love and deeds of courage are able to break the spell and change the princess back into her original shape.

In feeling our emotions, we bring them into the light of the heart, so that we come to understand the nature of them. The heart chakra is the organ of the soul. By bringing our emotions into the heart, their nature is transformed through the qualities of the heart. The heart seeks to love. In the flame of the heart, ugliness is transformed into something beautiful: compassion and understanding.

In the Grail myth, Parsifal is transfixed when the drops of blood fall onto the snow. This symbolises that his inner world now holds sway over him. His psyche is calling him. He is ready to serve his feminine principle. He realises how out of communion he is with his inner world. He is its abuser.

The feminine principle lives in us all, in the shape of the goose, in the shape of the Hag, not valued by the material world and relegated to a world of fantasy.

The rationalisation of our feelings is depicted in the Grail myth. One of the objects paraded before Parsifal in the castle of the Grail is *a sword cleft in two*. One half of the sword represents will and intellect and is an expression of the masculine principle. It is based on the law of force. The other half of the sword represents compassion and meaning and is an expression of the feminine principle. It is based on the law of love. Both sides of the sword must be brought together, fused and made whole again

Will and intellect enforced without understanding and compassion can only ever be a sword of destruction.

The headless knight, nursed in the arms of the weeping girl, symbolises that through the misuse of the sword, the young and inexperienced masculine principle has severed his head from his heart, intellect from feeling.

The weeping girl is another shape worn by Parsifal's feeling self. She weeps for Parsifal. Through ignorance, he has forged cleavage between masculine and feminine realities. Through their disparity, masculine and feminine are out of communion and all things fail to prosper.

Parsifal had been taught etiquette and knightly conduct. These were the skills that would enable his personality to meet the demands of the outer world. But all he had really learned was how to hack and dismember his head from his heart with more efficiency.

The sword cleaved in two also symbolises the polarity between men and women. When one part of the self is warring against another, it creates an inner dynamic that causes the outer disparity in our relationships. If we do not understand our own inner conflicts, we project them out onto each other.

In the symbol of the sword cleft in two, we are told that we need to bring the two sides of our nature together. How otherwise can we understand the true meaning of justice when we are as blinded to the inner world as the dead eyes of the beheaded knight? There is no such thing as objectivity as long as we are unconscious of the forces that live within the psyche. Our view of reality is limited, coloured and shaped by the dark side of all that is denied within us.

We look out upon our world judging reality only by what we can physically see. As long as we know not both sides of reality: outer as well as inner, masculine as well as feminine, we are unfit as judges, and unwise as kings. We are tyrants when in power, greedy when rich, victims when poor. Our world is ruled by ignorance.

Grail legends weave Solomon into the fabric of the collective myth. He represents the wise king and links western Grail myths with more ancient mythology.

The Parsifal story gives us another king in the image of *Arthur*. In him, we see another aspect of the masculine principle. Arthurian legends weave tales of how Arthur takes the sword from the stone and so reveals himself as the true king—the long-awaited one, worthy to rule over all of Britain.

This act symbolises the potential of the masculine principle to be a wise king of the inner realm. Excalibur is the sword of justice. Power is balanced by feeling.

But Arthur failed to ride out to recover the chalice stolen by the Red Knight. The recovery of the chalice, symbol of the feminine principle, was not considered important. Instead of setting out in its pursuit, he sent Parsifal, the fool, in his place. It was this act that eventually led to the downfall of Camelot.

Arthur represents worldly power, consciousness and outer control. But in failing to rescue his feeling self, he allowed a fool to take the place of a king.

After he was defeated, his mighty sword Excalibur was cast back into the lake. A hand reached up and took it down into the watery depths, which symbolise the feminine realm of the psyche. And there it still lies—masculine symbol of wisdom, buried in the depths of the feminine world.

All the characters in the Parsifal tale represent diverse aspects of masculine and feminine principles.

When Parsifal slays *the Red Knight*, it is a symbolic act of extreme denial. It signifies the suppression of anger, greed and lust for power. None of us want to face those things in ourselves, so we kill them off and drive them into shadow form. Whatever lives in shadow form as a result of denial is given more power. Eventually it always defeats us.

At first, Parsifal's pursuit of his goals is innocent, his desire natural and eager. However, he must earn his armour like the rest of men. His hungry ego is beginning to gain in strength. All his attention is bent upon its feeding. It is the armour that will protect him from the hard knocks that life will deliver. But it is worn like an actor's mask behind which he may hide his foolishness and his vulnerability.

Although he now assumes the outer appearance of sophistication, it is put on over the welsh tunic given him by his mother. This hair suit is still worn by the foolish boy who yet lurks beneath the armour of the Red Knight. The immature youth may have learned to remain well hidden, but still he is there: undeveloped, fragmented, and naive of the unseen forces that hold sway over him.

His act of boiling the body of the knight out of his armour is so inappropriate, so lacking in feeling, propriety or respect. The outer appearance of sophistication symbolised by his red armour does nothing more than hide his immaturity. Underneath it all, he is still a foolish boy parading as a man.

We should not face the world without any armour. This would also be foolishness. But in adulthood, we need to look behind our armour. We need to peel it off so that we know what lurks behind the smooth surface of a self-created and projected image.

The Red Knight is Parsifal's shadow. Outwardly Parsifal appeared so innocent, so foolish and completely ignorant of his own motivations. Yet he left a train of havoc in his wake and caused the wounding of the goose and the destruction of the woman in the tent.

Red represents desire and raw masculine power. And Parsifal must make a show of his power and possessions in the outer world in order to gain the approval of his peers. There was now no separation between Parsifal and the Red Knight. They were one and the same. The Red Knight was slain by a fool. While the fool, in turn, became the Red Knight.

When we deny our shadow, we become it.

The Hag accuses Parsifal of the sin of unconsciousness. This is the sin from which all others originate.

The Red Knight can be physically seen everywhere, riding through the halls of power, overriding feelings, denigrating experience, taking life by storm. The Red Knight is the seeker of materialism—the self-serving businessman—the rapist of the feminine world. He is *the-taker-out-of-life* and *the-leaver-of-nothing-for-anyone-else*. We see him manifesting in all his power and glory in areas of conflict around the world.

He also appears in acts of mental aggression. He is the energy behind intellectual prowess that tears feeling asunder, that belittles the non-rational world as being nothing more than superstitious nonsense. He tells us not to cry and despises the feeling world that would show emotion. Yet his own suppressed emotion keeps him an immature fool reacting in ways that may appear rational, but are demonstrative of the need for power divorced from feeling.

*T*he masculine spirit wears many different guises.

Duke L'Orguelleus de la Lande depicts the violence of the thwarted will. He is the spirit never softened by love. He cruelly punishes all that is feminine blaming her for that most ancient sin that caused his expulsion from the Garden of Eden.

She ate of the fruit of the tree of knowledge. She gained the power of that knowledge. She, representing the world of the soul, became conscious.

The soul seeks consciousness. It seeks to know itself.

The Church's teaching on the sin of Eve has given men unconscious permission to violate women. Their patriarchal and rigid male god has decreed that woman must be blamed for the original sin—the fact of incarnation—the fact of human suffering. The masculine spirit was forced thereby to become conscious of vulnerability, nakedness, and mortality.

He beats against his feminine soul to control her, to possess her, to make a show of his power in order to hide his vulnerability and nakedness. This is Lucifer's sin—the enormous sin of pride. It is to this energy— the raging fires of the thwarted will that we owe the rape and battering inflicted upon women the world over.

Deep within the woman, this distorted aspect of her own inherited and undeveloped *animus* storms against her, punishing her for the sin of Eve— for the fact of being a woman. She is forever trying to make up for it. She feels responsible for violent men, as if she is to blame for male wounding. All that is truly wounded is male pride. And pride is a vicious animal. It attacks in order to preserve itself.

One of the recurring psychological patterns in rape is that women feel guilty for having been raped. Our courts of justice, constructed of the masculine paradigm, reaffirm women's guilt. They find men not guilty of rape if the woman was considered to be wearing provocative clothing, or tempted the man into sexual embrace.

This is actually considered to be a valid *rational* argument. This could never be so if the spirit within our judges was not already violating their own feminine nature—unconsciously blaming it for their downfall and seduction. Deep down they give it no respect, no power, and no recognition, but seek only its domination and humiliation.

The tears of the weeping girl accuse Parsifal of his failure. Her knight was emotionally dead—his head separated from his heart. Parsifal had not asked the right question and thereby failed to heal the Wounded Fisher King.

To release the ailing king from his suffering had been the destiny bequeathed him by his bloodline. So when Parsifal sees *the drops of blood* fall onto the clean white snow, his ancient spiritual destiny stirs his blood. And his conscience appears to him in the shape of the Hag.

The three drops of blood remind him of the crucifixion. The cock crowed three times marking Peter's betrayal of Christ.

The purity of the snow signifies the virgin. The virgin portrays not the womb—but the pure in heart. The lost Grail chalice is the heart containing the legacy of Christ.

Parsifal betrayed his heart.

All that had beckoned him in the past, had been filled with meaning and numinosity, had eluded him. The sight of the knights in the forest had been enough to stir a passionate heart and arouse the sleeping spirit within. He had felt the fire of spiritual purpose of one destined to become a saviour. He would find some shining armour of his own and leave his mother's house and go in search of his destiny. Although he had no outer power, symbolised by the old nag who could not carry him far, he did have a secret power, something not given him by any circumstance other than that which pulsed through his veins. But he had allowed his spirit to become dissipated by worldly distractions and with it had achieved nothing of any meaning or value. He had become disillusioned.

When the soul begins to overlight the personality, it begins the tempering of the ego. This is an internal process, always involving loss and destruction.

In the Parsifal myth, this motif is depicted when Parsifal loses the Grail castle and the undervalued treasures of the spirit hidden therein. In one fell swoop of ignorance added to the already accumulated load piled against him, he tipped the scales of balance and lost all that would ever be of meaning and value.

The masculine principle must kneel before the feminine principle and sheathe the sword. He cannot enter the feeling world armed with logic.

He must become a spiritual knight, carrying out deeds of chivalry. He must put the feminine principle first. Using the power of his will to serve his heart, the power of his intellect to serve feeling and engender consciousness, he is able to penetrate the inner world—wherein dwells the Grail.

Through the surrender of the inner aggression against the Self, Parsifal is able to transform the shape of the Hag back into its original form. She becomes a highly developed feeling function. She will guide him through the undergrowth of the unconscious—the inner wasteland that must be crossed on his return journey to the Grail.

The Grail Chalice—container of the Blood of Christ—symbol of inner spiritual unity—signifies the spiritual consummation between masculine and feminine principles.

In this consummation the power of healing is bestowed.

Parsifal is the seeker of wisdom. He is the woman in search of her spirit—the man in search of his soul. Masculine seeking his intrinsic feminine self, feminine seeking her intrinsic masculine self—two halves of the one whole seeking the inner marriage.

Parsifal is the neophyte approaching initiation. He is the Red Knight extrovertly expressed in the outer world of materialism, or inwoven within the hidden feminine world of the psyche—playing out the drama of hero. He is the raw masculine energy of spirit—fool, red knight and king.

Ruthless, determined and unfeeling, Parsifal is a magnificent sword that must be tempered by love.

Twenty three

The Psychic Dance

Blanchflor and the Red Knight

The dead weight of the unspoken word hangs heavy in the atmosphere of childhood. The subtle ways in which we control each other are negative examples passed on to our children. These will instil in them equally negative patterns of behaviour that will be re-enacted in their future relationships.

Undercurrents of anger, resentment, guilt and blame—those are the unspoken hurts that engage partners in a *psychic dance*. The dance is one of fury. Its rhythm beats out the declaration of war on the opposite sex. This is the battlefield on which our children are weaned.

Though Blanchflor and the Red Knight may seem no more than fairytale motifs, when questioned deeply, they are icons of love relationships the world over.

Blanchflor represents Parsifal's anima. She is his most perfect ideal. But she also embodies a complex. This complex is not the prerogative of gender, but is intrinsically woven into the feminine psyche—woven also into the contra-sexual feminine nature of men.

Blanchflor personifies the wounded soul. The soul feels abandoned. It lives in a body that never knows, or recognises its value or meaning. Partners, therefore, relate to each other through a shared—although often denied—fear of abandonment.

Fear makes what is feared manifest. Our fear of abandonment is an inner saboteur. It generates all manner of emotional reaction such as possessiveness, jealousy, pride, and anger. These fear responses provide the means by which we make possible our own inevitable abandonment.

Blanchflor and the Red Knight depict the emotional drama of falling in love.

Blanchflor so willingly gives away her power to the knight in shining armour who will rescue her from the lonely tower that keeps her prisoner. And the energy that would otherwise have been spent in creative self-expression is focused wholeheartedly on attracting the beloved who can crash down those virgin walls and set her free.

Once freed, however, she realises that she has abandoned herself and is now merely a satellite in her lover's orbit. In craving his reciprocal attention, she has begun to live her life through him. Without a life of her own, she is doomed again to sit inside the dullest of towers, waiting on a word of praise, dependent on any sign of recognition that will empower her for a brief moment.

Deep within the feminine psyche, the urge to self-abandonment excites and overpowers. It expresses itself as a deep yearning to give over responsibility to the beloved. She wants to be rescued and dominated. This urge is closely connected to the mystery of female sexuality. It manifests outwardly as a sweet surrender to that special someone who will take care of her, make decisions for her, and take control. This kind of sexual attraction means she gives her power away.

The power of the Red Knight lives within the feminine psyche. It is a facet of the *animus*—contra-sexual nature of woman. Not only is the Red Knight an externalised force—expressed by men and women who ride roughshod over others imposing their will on all they meet—it also lurks within the feminine psyche as a hidden will-to-power—a ruthless will that dominates her own feeling, emotional reality.

When acknowledged, the spirit of the Red Knight within the woman is a positive force that will give shape and identity to her feminine nature. It is this spirit that gives her the drive necessary to achieve her purpose.

Spirit is energy. It all depends on which purpose it serves. When unrecognised, the Red Knight is made impotent through denial—changed into a ruthless psychic controller.

This wounded parody of spirit in her is transferred onto the man she falls in love with. She will look to him to go out there into the world and gain the things she wants, but cannot secure for herself.

Her needy dependency is heavy baggage to carry into any relationship. In those suitcases is the full weight of her desperation. In them glowers the dark secret of her craved recognition. She needs to be loved and made beautiful. She needs respect for her individual identity, for what she believes in, her talent, and her potential. But she depends far too much on her knight to give it to her.

Before that recognition comes naturally and unsought from others, she must first learn to give it to herself. The more she reaches out and asks the outside world for the recognition that she needs to build self-esteem, the more likely she is to be rejected. Usually this happens at a time when the teeth of her partner, or indeed anyone to whom she has transferred power, are sharpest, and can tear her more easily to pieces, and leave her bleeding from old wounds reopened.

In Blanchflor's imagination, the beloved has assumed godlike proportions. And because she has given him so much power, he automatically responds to the thing weakest in her. He either begins to despise it, or assumes responsibility for it. Her knight thus becomes ever stronger. She becomes weaker.

Rationally, she argues that she knows his faults. She makes excuses for them, cooing over such insignificant shortcomings affectionately. Then she sets about trying to change him—demanding that he respond to her emotional needs that have, in fact, been generated from her own lack of self-recognition.

The beautiful Blanchflor is gradually transformed into an accusing hag who nags and blames and makes demands that her knight cannot possibly fulfil. His inadequacy to meet his own emotional needs means he cannot meet hers.

She has fallen in love with his potential and sacrificed her own. It draws her. Suddenly, she has a purpose—she can make him into what she wants him to be. But what she wants him to be may be her own ultimate challenge—that which one day, she may become for herself. This challenge comes from within, imposed on her by her own spirit. But it has been unconsciously rejected for fear of failure, and projected instead onto the knight she falls in love with.

She may gain a convoluted sense of power from living through someone else's. But the power of the Red Knight burns with the passion and fury of a thwarted will. Secret desire is distorted into seeking an unconscious and unwholesome control over others.

In so devotedly seeing her knight's potential, Blanchflor has denied his reality. She does not hear what he really says, only what she hopes he says. Nor does she really know him. He is a projected fantasy of her own hidden power, of the undeveloped animus within her.

Her knight is the rescuer manufactured from her own unconscious. In him, she invests depths into which he will probably never dive, and sympathises with pain he will probably never feel. And whilst entrusting to him traits of character that are not his, but in fact her own, she prefers to dream of the day when he will give her the recognition she so badly needs. The more he denies her that recognition, the more she seeks it.

Moody men also exercise psychic control. Though highly emotional, their *anima* is weak—causing them to sulk and withdraw, rather than identify what they are feeling.

The underdeveloped feminine nature in men also causes them to feel needy and neglected. In turn, they give up their power to women. Negative emotions, such as desperation and insecurity, touch off the same in others. These are emotional demands—impossible to meet in each other.

Traditionally men are not allowed to own up to their weakness or vulnerability. Blanchflor—also molded by cultural expectations makes no exception. Seeing his weakness would burst her bubble of illusion. Her knight would have betrayed the power invested in him. He would be seen as weak and vulnerable and not godlike.

In order for Blanchflor to understand the vulnerability of men, she would have to peel off her own armour. She would find that her inner knight has abandoned her. She is weak in spirit and must accuse herself.

In the inner, unseen realms, her denied masculine spirit commits his crimes against her soul. By the wrong use of the sword, her inner knight has disconnected her head from her heart, and thus dishonoured and tortured her soul who speaks the language of feeling and meaning.

Though she does not know how to communicate her feeling self, she demands recognition for it. The beautiful Blanchflor must face her own denials, foolishness, sublimated ego and ruthless will.

Women and men together must liberate the feminine soul.

The soul is muse—bringing forth the gift of inspiration—the fruits of the non-rational world. She is the nurturer of spirit. Only she can temper the blade of will.

Blanchflor must go on her own quest for that which has meaning and value. But she is addicted to the knight through whom she lives a vicarious glamour. So she props him up and thus seals the secret bargain of denial.

The spark of love ignites into a burning passion only if her knight's power is something she wants. That power must remain elusive—taunting her desire to possess it. And in possessing it, she relieves herself of a heavy burden of responsibility. Learning to recognise and value her own potential—wherein lies her true power—would summon her own spirit to the rescue. Instead, it is condemned to burn in dark and secret places—a thwarted thing misshapen into violence against the self.

Meanwhile, the other partner in the dance makes his princess a secret promise that he will fulfil her. But he cannot do this because he has not yet fulfilled himself. He knows his deepest needs and motivations no more than she. He knows not how he is the betrayer of himself.

It is impossible for someone else to be responsible for the happiness of another. As soon as her knight assumes the role of making her happy, both players are immediately engaged in the game of denial. To be a player in this game demands that she never acknowledge her true feelings for fear of disappointing her partner. If she does, she takes the risk of blowing holes in his expectations of her and exposing a tattered wedding gown stitched together with conditions. Both partners will only keep their secret bargain as long as they support each other's unconscious emotional addictions.

Reality begins to awaken her from submissive complacency. She had limped into the relationship in the first place. In the cold stark light of reality, she begins to see this kind of love as no more than an emotional prop—a psychic crutch that supports issues and complexes. Indeed, it supports all the areas where growth is stunted. She can no longer play the game. The illusory light of infatuation has fizzled out. Her love has been tested in the dawn light of reality, when the sound of the crowing cock will see the betrayal of so conditional a love fulfilled.

He has seen her neediness exposed, and confirms her deepest fear of abandonment. All the reasons he was attracted to her disappear as if in a puff of smoke. The power once lent her is wrested back. Just one more hurt to fuel the bitter accusations of denial. Blanchflor and the Red Knight must accuse each other if they would keep their armour intact.

In the myth, Parsifal, as Red Knight, is depicted as being transfixed by the ultimate symbol of spiritual consummation between masculine and feminine spirits: red blood on white snow—the power of the spiritual bloodline superimposed on that which is virgin. This is Christ-blood in a virgin heart—the Holy Grail. Only now does the Hag have inner power enough to accuse him of his crimes against the feminine world—the abandonment of Blanchflor and also his mother. He must now see his actions proper only to the fool hidden within the mighty armour of the Red Knight. In order to have power and success in the outer world, he had betrayed his own soul.

He had not allowed the spirit of femininity to hold sway over him. Inevitably, she would betray him. She would become his inner saboteur who would rob him of his power. She would come to accuse him in the shape of the Hag. She would reach up out of the deep of his unconscious, to reclaim the sword of kingship, which the masculine spirit was found unfit to wield.

Abandonment and betrayal are the two faces of the same rune. If this rune has been cast, partners in the dance have already betrayed their inner selves and can know only abandonment and betrayal of each other. That which is denied within the unconscious acts as a powerful magnet. The abandoned seeks an abandoner—the betrayed, a betrayer. It is inevitable that they will find each other and when they do, they will fall in love.

It is always an equal dance, no matter how outward appearances may deceive. The betrayer is always at work within the psyche—the Judas who would betray love.

Parsifal had robbed the woman of her ring, plunging her into serious misfortune.

The ring is the self-renewing and everlasting feminine symbol of wholeness. With its circular shape that signifies no beginning and no end, it is complete within itself.

122

When Parsifal steals the ring from the woman in the tent—another facet of Blanchflor—he symbolises the innocent fool who blunders into the life of others wearing the shape of the rescuer. But he is really the robber of her tenuous identity.

Likewise, the rescued looks to persons more dynamic. Vicariously, they seek the power of the strong one and so lightly abandon their own. In this way, they project an impossible responsibility onto their saviour. Disappointment is inevitable.

Blanchflor is considered the perfect feminine ideal. She is virgin, untouched by her own spirit. Yet, she is also whore. She so lightly abandons herself to the lover who will save her from having to take any responsibility, not only for the choices she would make, but also for that which she might, one day, become. She remains the perfect partner only of an untempered and immature spirit.

Ever, they seek one another—two halves of one whole—destined to become submerged in each other's identities. Instead of first looking to the power of the feminine within him—to his own heart that would soften and nourish his spirit—the Red Knight seeks her from the outer world. He will not recognise her, for he has not come to know her within himself.

He takes by force, and not by understanding, that which will always elude him. But he cannot touch her inner being, only her outer skin, which he molds to fit the shape of his own hand.

While she must let her spirit ravish her, or be forever untouched, too soft, unshaped by purpose, power, or direction.

If wo-men never penetrate the shadow world, the inner self is always virgin. Both masculine and feminine natures remain unconsummated. The soul is never known—the spirit never tempered. Their unified purpose is never expressed in the outer world. Blanchflor and the Red Knight will continue to partner only the weakness in each other.

Fate has birthed identities born of empty sacrifice that cannot withstand being swept away by the power of the unknown opposite. The potential of the little budding self is abandoned to the rescuer who appears as the other half.

Inner ugliness, self-loathing and self-rejection motivate Blanchflor to choose which rescuer will share the marriage-bed. His task is to make her beautiful—thereby to give her power. She thus transfers her potential onto someone else, giving up her creativity, her genius, and her right to be whole.

Her knight is also busy transferring his inner woman onto his beloved. Projecting onto her fragile identity the face of perfection, he invests her with all the qualities that unbeknown to him, he needs to develop within himself. The woman he falls in love with is an outer projection of his own anima—a projected ideal, a fantasy woman not made of flesh and blood.

The bargain is sealed. The rescuer and the rescued have entered the dance. But they dance by the light of an illusory moon. In an abandoned choreography, they become easily enamoured with a partner who is but a projection of their own unrealised potential. The real person is never loved. For this choreography never permits the freedom of Selfhood. Each partner is a marionette of a lover's unconscious projections.

Blanchflor and the Red Knight dance not only with each other's glamours, but also with the psychic horror of each other's denials. She thinks the fancy dancer clever. He is able to outmanoeuvre her. But he is the devil dancer, come to rob her of wholeness.

There is an unconscious transference of energy. Very soon it becomes an energy drain. They are bound to each other as though with invisible tentacles that reach and probe for recognition deep into the other's emotions. Once embedded, they may suck and feed until the source runs dry.

This is a psychic vampirism that feeds a shared addiction. It is a partnership that dines on psychically transferred emotional demands that slowly poison and erode self-esteem. Self-esteem is eroded by guilt. Guilt is harboured in secret, as though it were a criminal. Deep down, they know they are abusing each other, and themselves.

Secret guilt always attracts blame. Blame stabs at hidden complexes and makes them bleed. Complexes grow fatter on this poisoned criticism. Complexes are always ready to believe the worst. How rarely are these partners receptive to each other's praise, gratitude, or respect! Their mutual complexes stand—sinister sentinels that prevent love from entering. And a budding heart that has waited too long to be nourished on a draught of love is shrivelled instead—twisted in the sour juice of bitterness.

Although invisible, these tortuous links make Blanchflor and the Red Knight prisoners of passion—holding them fast in a union of despair. This union is based solely on desire and sexual attraction. Rarely, in this dance is the heart involved. The heart only becomes active when love of a more unconditional and less immature nature is experienced. Below the waist, this couple now has one extended body. The psychic transference of energy has become a necessity. For some, this passionate interplay is not a problem. It is exactly what is craved—mutual emotional addiction. But this form of negative love can kill.

When transferred poisonous thoughts enter the sensitive feeling body, they cause disturbance and reverberations that are felt throughout the whole being. The circles of cause and effect, whether felt consciously or not, do their work. The complexes within must respond—they must fight in self-defence, or attack in retaliation.

Eventually, the fight manifests in the adrenal glands, which respond by pumping their poisons throughout the blood stream where they flow undigested into the organs of the body. The system of these individuals is always out of balance, prone to backache, headache, allergies, digestive problems, sudden depletion of energy and more serious diseases such as cancer, heart attack, or dependency on addictive substances that will dull emotional pain and substitute for a time, the emotional need.

Denial prevents the dive into the deep, cold waters that would heal. The trickery used by denial is indeed wizardry of an evil kind. Denial is always able to justify blaming someone else. Denial makes it possible for partners to give up their power to each other, to crave to be rescued, to want someone else to take responsibility, and when they do to scream abuse, disappointment and hurt.

In such a reaction, partners continue to lose themselves. They remain entangled in passion, rendered impotent to do anything other than to project blame onto each other. From psyche to psyche, back and forth, partners in the dance fruitlessly thrust and parry projected emotions. Underlying complexes that have generated those emotions will stay intact.

Very soon, those complexes succeed in their sinister molding of partners' outer shapes. These shapes are manifestations of each other's unconscious. Suddenly, the female partner has been turned into the mother, sister, or ex-wife. She is the silly goose, the hag, and the weeping girl. The male partner has been turned into the father, brother, or ex-husband. He is red knight, Duke L'Orguelleus, wounded fisher king.

The inner witch of denied emotion turns both partners into misshapen identities.

Denial responds only to denial. It creates horrible shapes that mold identities into its ugly form. The woman feels as if she were fighting some invisible force as the power of her beloved's denied projections so subtly molds her form and rapes her identity. Eventually, she becomes that which he makes her. Just as subtly, he is being transformed into that which she makes him. He is changed from prince to toad, until he can do no right in her eyes. In the beginning, she fell in love because of his familiarity. But all she really saw in him was the potential she denied in herself. Now instead of admiring it, she fights it. It has become a power issue—a way in which each partner struggles to control the other.

The ego is addicted to the things that support it—no matter how draining or detrimental to well being—no matter how much each partner may have to deny of themselves.

Severing the bonds that bind is an extremely painful experience. And no matter the distance, the psychic bonds we forge in negative relationships will never be broken, unless the energy that forged them in the first place is transformed. Only then will they loosen their hold and give room to breathe the sweet, cold air of freedom.

We are left with huge holes in the emotions. We try to fill them as quickly as possible. We crave satiation, and seek another relationship of similar kind. But this is the time to feel it all. This is opportunity for growth. If all the negative, hurt emotions are allowed to flow out along their natural channels, they lead to self-respect, not bitterness. Energy blocked is free to move. The bonds that have tied one to the other, have until now, whether pleasantly or painfully, bound up energy so that it flowed only in one direction, feeding only the one on whom it was focused. Now those links are broken. They hang limp and lost. And there is nowhere to go other than to enter the dark and terrifying void that threatens to swallow us all.

Twenty Four

The Negative Mother

The untempered spirit has no understanding of his own feminine nature. His little knowledge makes her a creature so alien. When he tries to enter into her realm, he is often consumed and overwhelmed by it. This creates the *Negative Mother Complex*.

Underneath the armour of the Red Knight, Parsifal still wore the welsh tunic given him by his mother. He may indeed have left his physical mother, and to all intents and purposes have made his own way in the world, but he had not yet left his *psychic mother*. Underneath it all he was still her son. She still possessed him—body and soul.

She is the dark matrix of fear and negative emotion.

This awesome collective power is given a metaphorical feminine identity. Based on an archetypal shadow force within the collective unconscious, this dark matrix gives rise to every feminine complex and extreme. It is the force that drives the Negative Mother Complex in men and in women.

Her possessiveness, fear, inertia, guilt and hatred wills to hold us in her dark womb. This womb is not life giving, but life suffocating. She will not set her children free.

Her insidious words are creatures that rise from the slime of the collective unconscious. They are *gremlins* that grow into monstrous, vicious little *imp-pulses* with lives of their own. They are inner enemies—saboteurs of individuation that come unbidden to rob us of spirit. We may think them quite harmless. We do not notice them because they are so familiar. But they are servants of a ruthless possession. They speak with her voice, urging in us self-hatred, self-doubt, insecurity and lack of trust in life.

Their ugly, discordant chaos distracts us away from the quiet voice of the soul.

The internal din of the Negative Mother rises from deep within our psyche. Her words artfully manipulate our thoughts to do her bidding. *"No, you can't,"* she says, *"You're not good enough."* Then, every urge or desire that is our own is snatched away, cast into the murky depths of self-doubting, where her thought-police keep us prisoners of a collective darkness.

Shoulds and Shouldn'ts, Do's and Don'ts prevent us thinking or living originally. Again she robs us of our strength and reason. Again and over again, we sink beneath the surface of consciousness into the realms of petty emotional reaction.

Mocking then at our confusion, she cries out, *"You should be doing something else."* We should always be doing something else; it is *never* good enough. She urges us to action—never allowing us to be still in case we become conscious for a moment of the power of her evil.

Her cracked and mirthless laugh screeches out. Once we hear her voice, every urge of spirit to be creative or express individuality is doomed. Her intention is to rob us of power and confidence. Consciousness must never gain enough strength to break free. Thus we remain in her possession. She shapes us in the mold of her created illusions. She defeats us at every turn.

Her emotional urgings grow like poisonous weeds. Her cacophonous words tell us of our failure and of our doom. Her voice sounds so reasonable as it demands, *"What have you got to offer?"* Or, *"You'll fail if you try,"* or *"What if it goes wrong?"* It is never difficult to believe her gremlin army with the pricking of their sharp little tongues. They never have to try hard to convince us that we are useless. As we already believe, due to the power of the collective to crucify the individual, that we are failures, unlovable, and have no value whatsoever.

Eventually, we become our gremlins. We take on their ugly shapes and live our lives expressing only their reality.

The Negative Mother constantly denies us our experience and victory. She eats her children then spits them out without identity. She denies us the right to try for ourselves. As soon as she is operating within the unconscious, we are unable to make decisions. Our sense of direction has been swallowed up—the fire of purpose and of commitment drowned in her oceanic depths to which there is no end. And no end either, to her seething emotionality and boiling resentments.

Love never enters her darkness.

She starves us of nourishment. She feeds us only on the negative psychological patterns that she has nurtured in us. We are driven by her ego to achieve only those things that will never satisfy. So the void is there, waiting to envelop us all.

But she is clever, always driving us to work harder, faster, better. We fear being still. We fill our empty lives instead, with distractions. "*Surely it is better to be distracted than to feel the void?*" we may ask. But this is the wheedling, beguiling voice of the Negative Mother.

This black widow makes us her feast. She spins her web around our unconscious, injecting us with the poison that will hold us fast. We are partially alive but unable to move. Caught in the threads of inertia, we die the slow death of unconsciousness. It is a death without rebirth. We are doomed to the hell spoken of in Biblical mythology. In this hell, she is free to feed off our confusion and inner turbulence. She is free to suck us dry so that we have not the strength to break free of her dark home within the unconscious. She has made it too comfortable a place to want to leave. In this hell, the dead bury the dead. We feel no pain.

She is the devouring, all-consuming mother of negativity—the archetype of the terrible mother feared by men and women alike throughout our mythological history. She is the Medusa who turns spirit to stone. She is inertia itself. Swallowed by her, we become lifeless matter— matter without spirit, life without meaning.

She devours ideas, feelings, original thoughts, hopes and visions. These are the children of the psyche. She eats them up before we've had the chance to give them birth. They are simply swallowed up by her raging jealousy that will not allow life to exist outside of her own. So many thunderbolts of inspiration are lost in the blackness of her boiling cauldron. So much of the fire of spirit is consumed to turn her waters red— red with insatiable desire—as the fires of hell.

129

Then she, who is the robber of creativity, births only the daughters of darkness whose names are jealousy and spite, resentment and hatred of life. They live in each of us, and in our mothers—their mothers also. And they live in the feminine nature of our fathers, husbands, brothers and sons. They are evil sisters—distorted emotions—the rotten fruit of the Negative Mother.

The will is also distorted by her insanity. Out of her, he is regurgitated the Satan—a hideous parody of the masculine spirit. Once, he was a dynamic offshoot of the power of creation. He was the first born of Agni—mythological god of fire—lord of the universe.

Lord Agni's son tried to penetrate his mother—like his father had. But she consumed him. Bound to matter for all time, he is Satan—the power that drives her desires.

This is the ancient curse of the mother that has left the men of this planet fearing being consumed by woman. Blaming her for the sin of Eve, blaming her for their own weakness, they fear penetration of her domain in case they are consumed by it. Will they lose control if they enter the feeling domain and be overwhelmed by an alien power?

The thunderbolt of power, offshoot of the lord of the universe, lost his life for penetrating his mother. Within the male psyche, the memory and the guilt lingers on.

Sexually, do men take women by force because of this ancient relic that lives within the collective unconscious? Is it a way to get even with the mother for consuming their power and rendering them impotent in the feeling world?

Perhaps the urge to rape is stimulated by jealousy of their father's power. Or perhaps it is jealousy of the secret power of the mother—a power they can never touch, never see, and never possess.

It possesses them, however, and consumes them, sometimes so obsessively that they project the Negative Mother onto all females. The inner unseen control drama is thus displaced—transferred instead to the outer world. Synchronistically, the dark Mother draws to us all the negative outer experiences on which she wishes us to feed. A lover appears to drive yet another nail into our self-esteem. We hear in them, the voice of criticism, the voice of accusation, reiterating the inner script.

This mother and her consort son are ancient relics of a greater evil. They reign supreme over the collective unconscious and lurk in the depths of each individual psyche. Their power is a negative planetary force that is anti-life. It draws us ever down sucking us back into the womb of unconsciousness.

With the power of her consumed lover, the Negative Mother rides us ever faster to be better and better. She whips us with the lashings of her mutterings. Secretly, they burrow into our psyches until they undermine the depths of our hearts. We are useless, so must always try harder, spending our lives driven towards some impossible goal that only exists in the world of illusion. Every time we approach it, the goal pops as a meaningless bubble pierced with the pinhead of dissatisfaction. Finally, her words drive us over the edge of the struggle and into her domain— into the dark, terrifying abyss of emotional despair from which there is no escape.

Her power works always through the collective, through ignorance and denial, through hatred and suspicion. It is the supreme power on earth.

The Negative Mother is not the Hag. The Hag comes to accuse us of our denial and unconsciousness. She begins the awakening process, when we are ready to own our own abuse of the feminine world. She seeks to make us conscious.

The Negative Mother seeks to keep us unconscious.

In the myth of Adam and Eve, Satan is said to have appeared disguised as the snake. He tempted Eve into eating the fruit of the tree of knowledge. In the ancient wisdom teachings, the snake is the symbol of knowledge. The Church has interpreted the symbolism of the snake to suit its own ends. It has been made a sin to become conscious, to have knowledge, to know ourselves as gods incarnated in wo-men. The Church— called by its Initiates, *Mother Church*—has conditioned us into remaining ignorant and unconscious. Its control is insidious. Its voice is made to appear as if it were the voice of wisdom, authority and goodness. It has appropriated many of the sacred myths and distorted their meaning in order to dominate, indoctrinate and control through fear. This attitude echoes the voice of the Negative Mother.

When women had knowledge in the past, they were called witches and burnt at the stake.

We have only to see the evil perpetrated by the Spanish Inquisition to know how the established Church preferred to destroy life rather than liberate it.

The excuse-makers are born from the dark womb of the Negative Mother. They rationalise atrocity, justify violence and reason with ogres. They tolerate little sins saying they are of no importance. But little sins pile up behind them. Suddenly they cast a giant shadow that blocks out the sun. Again, her mocking laughter—again we are plunged into another crisis. To keep the world on the constant brink of crisis is one of her aims. It allows us no time to breathe, no time to enjoy being alive, and no time for personal and social development.

In complacent reluctance to growth and change, we remain this mother's children. Only ever then are we the children of collective unconsciousness, of ignorance and immaturity. We are walking dead who have never lived lives of our own and will never know the childlike innocence that continuously renews itself on the miracle of life.

Her mighty bubble surrounds us. Collectively we cannot see outside of her reality. It contains us all. Thus, manifestations of her possessive control appear to most as normal.

Parsifal will never become the Grail knight as long as he is possessed by her negative psychic control. He must leave home for the second time and fulfil the potential of his spirit.

Book Five
Revelation

Twenty Five

The Cave of Treasures

One night I dreamed I saw a cave. In the dream, I was told it was the Cave of Treasures. I was instructed to remember this name. I was not to enter the cave but to follow the outside of the rock with the palm of my hand. The rock had been split asunder so that a casket could be buried inside. I followed the curve of the rock until I came around behind it and discovered a garden of paradise. The existence of the garden surprised me, but I realised that it had always been there. There was a house, which I knew to be the house of my ancestors. I entered in. Every wall was covered in miniature icons. I knew they were imprints of my ancestors. One was of a man with one eye. He stared at me and told me we were strongly related. There was a fierce and vital attraction between us. Three women were singing and sewing. They told me it was my house, and they were keeping it clean for me.

Sometimes, God comes forth in dreams.

Upon waking, I was excited by this dream. By profound coincidence, I discovered little-known academic writings on the Cave of Treasures. Prior to this dream, I had never heard of the *Cave of Treasures* and realised that I had dreamed of early Christian works that could be Ethiopic! My psyche was leading me deeper into the Grail myth, into the spiritual mystery of our ancestors and how they are always inextricably woven into our lives.

Should I have discovered these writings previous to dreaming their contents, they would have appeared merely academic. In the act of having dreamed them, and without prior knowledge of their existence, I emotionally experienced their profound significance.

By the grace of *Amrita*, I felt compelled to synthesise those early myths into a coherent whole. *Amrita* illuminated the essence of their meaning as follows:

After the fall, Adam and Eve saw their animal bodies.
They saw their nakedness, vulnerability and mortality.
They were ashamed of what they saw.
They knew pain, cold and hunger.

God gave them a place on the western edge of paradise
to be their abode.
They took shelter in the darkness of a cave,
where they could hide from the sight of themselves.
They lost consciousness in the dense darkness of the body.
They forgot who they were and from whence they had come.

They were the first cave men.

And God gave them treasures.
The treasures were golden staffs or rods, incense and myrrh.
These would stir their consciousness
and remind them of their spiritual home.

Adam and Eve called their home the Cave of Treasures
because of the gifts God had given them.

The golden staffs symbolised the threefold fire of Heaven.
This fire would kindle the spirit
and remind them of whence they had come.
It would illuminate their cave
and develop in them the gift of inner sight.
It would sustain their bodies
by giving them the gift of physical fire
with which to cook their food.

God told them the myrrh was for use in medicines
to heal the sickness of the soul.
It was also to be used in burial.
It would symbolise mourning.
It would remind them of the soul incarcerated
in the darkness of the body.
It would symbolise their journey through the valley of tears.

Myrrh would also remind them that God would come down:
a conscious soul incarnating in physical form.
God would send the son of Spirit
who would be crucified and buried,
and whose body would be embalmed with myrrh.

Man would mourn the crucified god.
And God would mourn the crucified man.

Incense was to remind the spirit of its benediction.
It would dedicate the spirit to returning from whence it had come.

Myth has it that Adam charged his son Seth to embalm him after his death. He was to lay his body together with the gold, incense and myrrh in the Cave of Treasures until after the flood—after which his body was to be placed in a ship. He was to be buried at the centre of the earth. From there, God would come and save the entire race.

Noah's son Shem is said to have eventually carried out this request.

Twenty Six

The Secret Name

Syrian legend tells how Melchizedek would accompany Shem on his journey. When they came to the centre of the earth—the place designated for the burial of Adam's coffin—Melchizedek would remain there as guardian of the sacred grave.

Historically, however, Melchizedek was not yet alive at the time of Noah. He appeared much later, during the time of Abraham, as the renowned king of Salem. His name meant king of righteousness.

After Abraham's victory over his enemies, legend has it that Melchizedek came to bless him and to offer thanks with bread and wine. This offering was a symbolic ritual performed only by *priests of God Most High.*

Scholars are not sure of Melchizedek's origins. Salem means peace. He is portrayed, therefore, as a king of peace and also a priest of God Most High. Thus he appears as a mystical pre-Christ figure. The New Testament states how this priesthood was not determined by the regulation of ancestry, but on the basis of the power of an indestructible life. For it is declared, "You are a priest forever, in the order of Melchizedek."

Melchizedek was said to be without father or mother, genealogy, beginning of days or end of life. S/he is the spiritually chosen one—named only by God. Thus s/he remains a priest forever.

Jesus also broke bread and drank wine at the Last Supper—a ritual that was to herald the *New Covenant.* In this act, he shows himself to be of the mystical order of Melchizedek.

The name Melchizedek does not belong to one person. *Amrita* revealed that this name belongs to an ancient order of souls. Thus does the spiritual bloodline of Christ continue to incarnate through Initiates who die upon the inner tree and are reborn into the indestructible life of Spirit.

They are the spiritually chosen, given a secret task for which only God names them.

Twenty Seven

When the hill shall be

split asunder

uring the journey to the centre of the earth, Adam spoke to Shem and Melchizedek from the casket.

Adam told them:

The Word of God will come down unto the land, which is our destination and will suffer and be crucified in the place where my body shall be buried. The crown of my head will be baptised with His blood and salvation will then be accomplished. My priesthood, my gift of prophecy and my kingship will then be restored unto me.

When they arrived at the place, the rock split asunder indicating the place where the casket was to be buried.

The splitting asunder of the rock is a recurring theme throughout Biblical mythology. When the children of Israel crossed the Sinai desert, Moses struck the rock three times. Water flowed out—symbolising setting free the soul of Israel from Egyptian bondage. This symbolic action symbolised that individually and collectively, the children of Israel would have to break the Covenant with the past.

The Ark of the Covenant stood upon a rock in the Temple of Solomon. At the moment Christ died on the cross, the curtain of the temple veiling the Ark of the Covenant in the Most Holy Place was rent asunder. The earth shook and the rock split, heralding the ending of the Old Covenant (outgoing Age of Aries) and the inception of the New Covenant (Age of Pisces).

The motif of the rock splitting asunder is also a recurring theme through the Grail myth. As Joseph made his way to Britain, many came to seek counsel from his marvellous legendary chalice that was said to possess mystical powers. Only the pure in heart could be in its presence. Those who were false in nature suffered a drastic fate. The ground opened up and swallowed them!

Twelve Knights were seated at the Round Table. The thirteenth seat was left vacant. It symbolised the place vacated by Judas at the Last Supper. Only the long awaited lost son destined to find the Grail would take this place. If a false saviour sat upon the thirteenth seat, he would meet his doom. The stone upon which the seat was placed would split asunder. Impostors would be swallowed whole.

The vision of the man asleep in the hill had begun my Grail Quest. It felt as if the process could not be halted as my psyche delivered up its secrets. These were the secrets of the soul. The revelation of one mystery guided me to the next—deeper and deeper into esoteric layers of meaning, back in time to civilisations long buried—to the inception of the Age of Pisces. I had been shown that when the rock had split asunder, it was in order that the casket may be buried—the secrets of the past inhumed. There they would remain for an Age awaiting the time when the *hill shall be split asunder and give up its find...*

Thus at the inception of the Age of Pisces, seeds of a new Aquarian dawn had already been sown.

The day I had ascended the Tor, I had visioned what I later realised to be the fulfilment of Adam's prophecy. Those ancient secrets would again be delivered up when: *the hill shall be split asunder.* The hill is the Chalice Hill—symbol of the Aquarian Heart. It is the rock that shall be split asunder. The Covenant with the past shall be ended. A new Covenant with Spirit shall begin that will open and awaken the human heart.

And he *shall be seen to be whole, uncorrupted by time, and shall change the world forever.*

These words mean that the Bloodline of Christ—of the order of Melchizedek, shall make themselves be known. These are the true priests and priestesses, prophets and rulers of the kingdom of spirit.

And they shall reign on earth.

Twenty Eight

Shambhala

dam bid his descendants to take him to the centre of the earth. Buddhist esoteric teachings describe the centre of the earth as the place where the four quarters of the earth come together—where the power of God stands still. This place is known as *Shambhala*, and is thought to be the heart chakra of the planet from which the forces of light are radiated out to the world. Sanat Kumara—the manifestation of God on earth is said to reside there.

The four quarters of the earth also signify the four arms of the cross. Whilst the numerical value of four is significant in many ancient philosophical systems of thought, the cross is a relatively modern Christian symbol. The cross therefore encapsulates the ancient ideal that there are four aspects or directions of Being. These belong to each of the four elements. These are earth, air, fire and water. Each of these symbolises a *Principle*—a basis for action—a function of being.

In the Grail Myth, these functions and elements of Being are represented by the *spear, sword, chalice* and *stone*. The spear dripping blood symbolises the function of intuition; it is of fire—and symbolises the spirit—the sudden knowing that comes from the world of archetypal idea. The sword made whole represents the function of thinking; it is of air—and symbolises the illuminated mind. The chalice represents the function of feeling; it is of water—and symbolises the soul and its expression in the heart, wherein heaven and earth, god and humankind, masculine and feminine are reconciled. The stone represents the function of sensation; it is of earth—and symbolises the body that will be ravished by spirit.

The Grail myth describes how the same spear that wounds is the same spear that heals. Love hangs us on the cross, only love can take us down.

If love is the motivating force that drives the Initiate into the underworld in order to cleanse her/his bloodline issues, the Initiate eventually comes to the centre of being. This is the fifth point—the sanctified heart. This is the *Shambhala* of inner being—the sacred place within—the *Sanctum*

Sanctorum where the functions of intuition, thinking, feeling and sensation come together and radiate their grace. During the initiation process, all four quarters of being have been purified—made whole. The Initiate stands free at the centre of the heart—the fifth point, in a state of dynamic inner stillness.

These five points symbolise the Star of David. The Initiate has been cleansed by the Blood of Christ, is now of the spiritual Bloodline of Christ, of the House of David—mystical order of Melchizedek.

The Initiate has died upon the inner tree. S/he has pierced the veil that separates the worlds and entered into the Spirit realm. In so doing, the Initiate has atoned for the sins of the fathers. In breaking the Old Covenant with the past, future generations will manage real and significant change from those ancestral thoughtforms that have kept the bloodline in bondage. The bloodline has produced a saviour of its own. This is the long awaited one—the child who has redeemed the sin of Judas, betrayer of the heart. This is the child of the generation who would penetrate the darkness of her/his own unconscious, descend into the inner hell, and do it in the name of love.

As Christ had done, who after His crucifixion descended into hell and set free Adam and Eve who were His ancestors. They were the first awakening souls incarnating into the darkness of the body. They were souls made wo-man—of the same nature as Christ.

God had taken Eve from within Adam. She was always within him, as he was in her. *Anima and animus* were thus split and fell out of communion with paradise. "Saved by the Blood of Christ," does not mean saved by a Christ who died two thousand years ago, but by the living legacy of Christ—symbolised by the Grail Chalice—in which masculine and feminine spirits are re-unified, raised again to the kingdom of Spirit.

Twenty Nine

The Fixed Cross

Four astrological signs constitute what esoteric astrologers describe as the *Fixed Cross* of the Zodiac. These signs are Aquarius, Leo, Taurus and Scorpio.

Inherent in this cross, astrological *oppositions and squares* give rise to tension, difficulty and struggle. Aquarius and Leo, Taurus and Scorpio are positioned opposite each other in the great zodiacal wheel. In esoteric astrology, when signs are opposite each other, they are considered to be shadow signs of each other.

The shadow sign of an Age is as important as the sign in which the Age openly expresses itself. The shadow sign influences the unconscious aspects of that Age. Therefore, in the Age of Aquarius, Humanity will play out its unconscious soul-making drama in the sign of Leo, when again, it mounts the Fixed Cross of the Heavens and plays out a new theatre choreographed and directed by the gods.

In Greek mythology, Hercules performed twelve labours. Esoteric Astrology defines these labours as spiritual tasks performed in each sign of incarnation. Although in Aquarius, our task is to clean out the Aegean stables by redirecting the two rivers—or streams of soul-force—symbolising the raising of the Kundalini—Hercules' labour in Leo reveals the way in which we shall face our shadow and thus achieve its Aquarian expression:

The Nemean Lion had devastated the population. Its skin was said to be invincible. Since no mortal could defeat it, Hercules was called to the task. To find and defeat the Lion, Hercules was forced to follow it into its lair deep inside a cave. The cave had two openings. No matter how Hercules stalked the Lion, it managed to escape unseen. Hercules realised that he must close off one of the exits. He must trap the Lion inside its lair. As weapons were of no use against this beast, Hercules slew the Lion using only his bare hands.

The Nemean Lion is the inner beast. It symbolises the wilfulness, desires and rage of the egocentric, infantile personality. These violent responses come from the unconscious (the cave). The Lion escapes the cave through the secret door to the unconscious—the alta major chakra.

The alta major tree has its roots in the base chakra, which rules adrenal responses. The base chakra is the seat of deep and undifferentiated violent passion. Hercules' task is to trap the Lion inside the cave. He must block off the hidden exit, so that his passions do not spill out and savage those around him. Then he must penetrate the front entrance of the cave in order to confront the Lion. The front entrance of the cave is a metaphor denoting the brow centre. The brow centre is ruled by the pituitary gland and is the seat of consciousness.

The pituitary gland is the governing gland of the endocrine system. Entering the cave this way means we bring the light of consciousness to bear on hitherto uncontrollable shadow urges that devastate others. Hercules will slay the Lion with only his bare hands. This signifies that Hercules will kill the Lion with only his strength of character and redirected *will-infused* consciousness.

After Hercules slew the Lion, he skinned it. Thereafter he wore the Lion's skin. This signifies the beast is integrated not denied. Hercules' spirit is thus made invincible.

Leo is the sign through which the soul will individuate. Leo rules the heart. The soul will individuate through the awakened heart.

The keynote of Aquarius is brotherhood and service. As individuals, we must collectively focus our consciousness in the heart. The human chain must become precisely that—forged in the spirit of unity and mutual respect.

The earth is not yet a sacred planet. Humanity must sound its note in the octave of universal vibrations. It is destined to be the manifestation of the Body of Christ. Humanity has yet to take its place in the Zodiac—on the thirteenth seat left vacant awaiting Heaven's lost Son.

Thirty

The Redemption of Eve

*T*he Ark of the Covenant contained four sacred things: *Moses' tablets of the law, Aaron's rod, golden candelabra, and the urn*, which was said to contain manna from heaven. These four things symbolise the threefold Blessed Trinity and its relationship to Humankind.

The tablets of Moses symbolise the Father Principle and spiritual lawmaker. Aaron's rod symbolises the Son of the Father, or Christ Principle. The golden candelabra symbolise the light of the Holy Spirit—the Mother Principle. And the sacred urn containing manna from Heaven is the sanctified human heart in which all three aspects of the Blessed Trinity meet and radiate their grace. Grace is the manna from heaven that will bring healing and spiritual nourishment to land, bloodline, culture and creed.

These motifs of the Blessed Trinity and its relationship to Humankind are resurrected in the Grail myth—the Chalice contains the *three persons of the one godhead.* Its relationship to Humankind is embodied in the *blessed woman who will give us counsel.* She symbolises matter that is sanctified—the human body—the physical expression of spirit.

Aquarian seekers must integrate the three persons of the one godhead in the heart and radiate such grace. The Grail is not an object to gain, but something we become. Such individuals will be Feminine Christs—not born of the womb, but of the sanctified heart. Thus s/he will be without father or mother, genealogy, beginning of days or end of life. S/he will be a priest forever, in the order of Melchizedek, of the spiritual bloodline of all those Christs who went before and will come again.

Amrita revealed to me how Aquarian seekers shall integrate the threefold fire of the down-pouring Blessed Trinity only through a *threefold initiation*—in *water,* which is the baptism of the emotions—in *blood,* which is the baptism of the soul and bloodline—and in *fire,* which is the baptism of spirit.

This threefold initiation may be experienced over a long period of time. Individuals may feel a slow burning in the head centre. This burning may over-stimulate emotional response and greatly exacerbate emotional events. Having journeyed across the wasteland of inner being, those of us called to the portal of initiation realise the full weight of our transgressions against the soul. We dissolve our sins in tears of self-forgiveness. This is the first baptism—in *water*. Tears baptise the emotions and enable us to awaken to the world of feeling and meaning. Energies from the *solar plexus* are raised into the heart. The heart becomes the centre wherein the life of the individual is focused. During this process, the astral body is vastly expanded and becomes an emotionally pure receptacle of soul experience. The heart is thus prepared for the second baptism.

Although personal pain is catharsised, the heart leads us into the deeper ancestral psychological thoughtforms that keep the soul in bondage. This is the baptism in *blood,* when the bloodline is purged and the sins of the fathers will no longer be visited upon the daughters or sons. The heart is split asunder—washed clean by the Blood of Christ. The purified heart is the Chalice now embodied in the Initiate. It will guide the seeker to the third baptism.

The Initiate now recognises the sacred vibration of her or his own secret name. S/he has come at last to the sacred place—to the centre of the heart where the four quarters of being stand still. This stillness cannot be achieved by an act of will or visualisation. It is born only of inner baptism, sacrifice and real transformation.

The Spirit descends only in response to the call of the awakening soul.

The soul will continue to overlight its vehicle of expression. Eventually it calls out to the One Initiator to stretch forth the rod of spiritual fire and strike the chord of sudden knowing. This kind of dynamic thought is born only of the impelling silence in which the inner thinker thrives. It comes from the world of idea—is felt in the centre of being where the power of God stands still. In that stillness is salvation for Adam and all his descendants accomplished. This is the baptism of *fire*—the consecration of spirit.

The chord reverberates throughout the Initiate. It tunes up her or his whole being, bringing all dissonance into alignment. Energy trapped is set free. Each of the chakras is opened and illuminated. From octave to octave, they sound their notes of perfect harmony.

The Apocalypse cryptically describes the *opening of the Seven Seals*. It also describes how John the Divine saw *Seven Spirits sit before the throne of God*. In this symbolism is hidden the mystery of initiation. The Seven Seals are the chakras, which must open to the light of the Seven Spirits. The Seven Spirits are the seven great cosmic archangels. When their perfection shines on the seven chakras, it brings imperfection to the surface. Archaic remnants sealed in the murky depths of unconsciousness spill out like plagues.

This process happens naturally. It is unwise to call it forth. This is each individual's Apocalypse. And only the awakened heart can transform it.

Different schools teach the opening of the chakras and subsequent raising of the Kundalini with breathing exercises or the use of visualised Colour. The Kundalini can only be safely raised with painstaking spiritual discipline involving first, the awakening of the heart. This process involves taking consciousness into the body from the head centres downwards—and then only when called to the task by the soul. As each chakra opens it is connected to its corresponding World Chakra. Thus the seeker would be foolish to begin from the root chakra and work up the spine without first having purified the heart! If this were the case, the Kundalini would dramatically burn through the etheric web leaving the seeker with no protection from the full force of the world's undifferentiated primal root chakra energy. This psychic refuse would destroy the Initiate, causing insanity or disease. Only character, courage and consciousness focused in the heart can withstand the opening of the Seven Seals, when the forces of the underworld shall spew forth inherent plagues caused by ancestrally inherited violation of the soul.

The Initiate must consciously journey into each of the chakras in esoteric order and purge the thoughtforms that hold the soul enthralled.

Amrita instructed me to reveal the esoteric order of the opening of the chakras. *Never has the secret mystery of the raising of the Kundalini been written. Only one who has, in truth, passed through this process, can know it...*

The fire of spirit baptises the crown chakra—known also as the Thousand Petalled Lotus. The pineal gland is vitalised. Energy of the greater Will pours in through the head centre—into the brow centre, and stimulates the pituitary gland.

When Christ spoke to Joseph during his confinement in prison, He told him: "*As the trunk bore the apple that grew from the tree by the miracle of God, so too had the Son of God to die upon the wood, in order to accomplish this salvation.*"

The apple that grew by the miracle of God refers to the pituitary gland stimulated by the down-pouring threefold fire of Spirit. It rules the third eye. When fully awakened, this is the eye of the heart by which the Initiate will see into Spirit realms. The Initiate thus enters in. S/he will also die upon the inner tree in order to be reborn into the life of Spirit. The inner tree is the alta major, whose roots burrow deep into the root chakra, with branches reaching up to the crown. This is the *tree of knowledge* upon which the Initiate stands alone in order to accomplish salvation for the bloodline.

Avalon was known as the *Island of Apples*. Perhaps this metaphor referred to Initiates who entered the inner realms via the Avalon of their own beings and awakened the third eye. They became ancient keepers of the secret knowledge—priests forever in the order of Melchizedek—the true spiritual Brotherhood of Christ.

The pituitary is the kingly gland that rules our threefold mental, emotional and physical being. When stimulated by the down-pouring fire of Spirit, it discharges elixirs into the blood stream. This is the elixir of life—the healing promised to those who find the Grail. These elixirs purify the blood. The blood will carry them to stimulate all other glands in the endocrine system. The secretion of those elixirs signals the endocrine system to set in motion a process that will open the chakras and raise the Kundalini.

This process can be arrested at any time if the Initiate does not remain conscious of her or his process. S/he must continue to cry—to release energy drawn to the surface by the fire of spirit. This process should not be blocked. To do so would cause over-stimulation of the chakras and lead to very unwholesome results.

The greatly increased activity of the pituitary gland first begins the opening of the alta major chakra. The carotid gland governs the condition of the alta major which rules the spine. During the slow process of initiation, the alta major projects the fire of down-pouring Spirit into the channel situated on the right-hand side of the spine. This channel, or nadis, is known as *Pingala*. As the fire of illumination penetrates deeper into the chakras, the psychic refuse of our ancestral lives is gradually discharged upwards flowing up the channel on the left-hand side of the spine known as *Ida*.

The alta major is the gateway to the emotional/astral world—the back door to the unconscious. The next chakra that will open therefore is the solar plexus, which is the seat of emotion. When the fires of illumination penetrate the solar plexus, our emotions are raised into the heart. They pierce the heart from below rupturing the heart's etheric web.

The heart centre now begins its full awakening. It become more inclusive and expansive and attuned to world suffering. It becomes the central force of our being. Acting as a magnet, it begins the slow and painful turn of direction that will draw the primal energy of the lower chakras up into consciousness. All the energy of the lower worlds must be transmuted through the heart.

The heart raises sexual energy from the sacral centre. This is the next centre to be vitalised. The Initiate penetrates ancestral miasma. Sexual energy is transmuted via the heart and raised to the brow centre. It feeds and strengthens the third eye that its vision may penetrate the deeper sentient desire worlds.

Eventually, the fires of illumination reach deep into the energy dormant in the root chakra. Only when the heart is the centrifugal force of being, is it safe to experience energy from this centre. It is unnameable—deep dark impotence—ancient yearning. This is the yearning of the spirit trapped in the desire world—the fallen angel seeking its redemption.

It is the primal consciousness of the body.

Situated beneath the base of the spine in the root chakra is coiled the sleeping serpent fire known as *Kundalini*. She is the mother who has dominion over the latent energy of substance itself. She rules all things physical, and has dominion over the world of instinct, survival and desire.

When touched by the fire of spirit, the coiled serpentine energy of the mother awakens. This is the snake that tempted Eve to desire consciousness.

Her fires snake up the spine through the central channel of *Sushumna*. She burns through the remainder of the etheric web. Her fires combine with the waters of the astral world. The desire nature has already been purged—the astral body greatly expanded.

Her fires are raised heavenward to the crown centre where she unites with the energy of Spiritual Will. When combined with the fires of down-pouring Spirit, she illuminates us with knowledge of past and future. This is the *Conjunctio* referred to by alchemists. Matter is raised heavenward and unites with the threefold nature of the one godhead. Raising the feminine spirit latent in matter to consciousness makes the mother blessed. She is the *blessed woman who will give us counsel.*

In Biblical mythology, the uncorrupted body of Mary, mother of Christ was raised into heaven after her death. This image was taken literally by the Church. It is however symbolic of the raising of the Kundalini. Matter—from the Latin *mater*—means mother. It is raised heavenward and thus redeemed. All the centres are vitalised. All limitations are destroyed. The Initiate stands perfected—God and human reconciled.

The third eye is fully opened. *The crown of the Initiate's head has been baptised with His blood and salvation is accomplished.* The Initiate has gained the gift of prophecy, priesthood and kingship. S/he is a true seer—a *priest of God Most High* in the order of Melchizedek. S/he hears the voice of God speak her or his name. This name carries the vibration of a sacred task for which the Initiate is named only by God.

S/he is touched by an archetype—destined to live out a myth. S/he will stand on the earth as a conduit through which in-pouring spiritual light comes to ground. The raising of the Kundalini creates a vacuum in the etheric web. The Initiate has left an empty space. By the laws of physics, it must be filled.

The Initiate's consciousness acts as a magnet that draws the energy of the collective unconscious into the vacuum. The vacuum serves as an open channel that constantly fills with the suffering of the world. The Initiate feels it all. From there the sins of the world are transmuted through the greatly expanded heart of the Initiate who is now functioning as a living Christ.

The Initiate is a link between Heaven and Earth. Through her or his intercession, Spirit is invoked that will come to meet the call of earth. The consciousness of the collective will gradually be raised—earth's vibration gradually more attuned to cosmic being.

Thus the *Feminine God* shall be made manifest for the first time in the history of the human race. She shall be the god of woman—born of the feminine paradigm—the world of feeling, meaning and compassion. Through her, men and women the world over shall be made blessed. And the New Covenant shall be fulfilled.

A New Rainbow Covenant

Then Amrita, who was the voice of my heart, spoke again.

Myths are parables
that speak in tongues
of universal lives
out of which human consciousness is molded.
You are the physical expression of those lives.
You live in them
as they live in you.
You move in them
as they move in you.

They are the great angels who influence the zodiac,
who have blazed their trail across the heavens,
and charted the journey each soul must make.
Turning the wheel of incarnation,
the angels bequeathed you their myths:
heavenly maps
that guide each lost and wandering soul home.

Their myths are allegories of the inner life.
Their imperfections,
the sins that keep you on the cross of suffering.
You, the weary travellers
seeking resolution
must work out the sins of those angels
the first born of His spirit.

In your human world,
you must atone for them.
Thus, shall the spirit be baptised.

They are avenging angels
doing battle with their own shadows.
In a revelation,
John the Divine saw them stand,
Seven Spirits before the Throne of God

Amrita bid me know the words of John the Divine from the Book of Revelations...

And he turned to see the voice that was speaking to him.
And having turned,
he saw seven lamp stands,
And in the midst of the seven lamp stands,
he saw one like to a son of man,
clothed in a garment reaching to the ankles,
girt about his breasts with a golden girdle.
In His right hand were seven stars.
Out of His mouth came forth a sharp,
two edged sword.
And His countenance was like the sun shining in its power.

He spoke to John saying,
"As for the mystery of the seven stars,
and the seven golden lamp stands:
The seven stars are the angels of the seven churches.
And the seven lamp stands are the seven churches."

Amrita spoke of the Seven Spirits before the Throne...

They are the seven great channels
through whom the divine being flows.
Their lord is the creator of the universe,
the great fire god
of power and will.
As seven spears,
He sent His cosmic angels
to pierce the silent void
that He may come to know Himself in form.
They shone forth to the seven stars
illuminating them with the Will of Heaven.
The seven stars are the Pleiades.

The Pleiades are the luminaries of the seven churches.
The seven churches are the sacred planets.
The seven sacred planets
are the luminaries of the twelve signs
of the zodiac.

And the light they shone cast up a shadow.
And he was an evil lord, capricious and ruthless,
the father of the twelve.
And the father of all
liked not His own darkness.
A great battle began.
And the father of the universe
fought all that brooked His path.

Worlds were created and destroyed.
Angels were cast to earth
and all substance was tainted
with their limitations.

And the Word was made flesh.
And He who was the Son of God
and yet the son of wo-man
was given twelve labours to perform,
to atone for the sins of the capricious angels
who were as gods.

Thus the seven perfect rays
who are the angels
of the seven colours of the rainbow
shine upon the seven sacred centres of man,
illuminating substance
already tainted with the sins of the fallen angels.

The seven sacred centres of wo-man
are the seven churches of wo-man.
They are the seven chakras,
waiting to open to the will of heaven
as though they were lotus flowers
blossoming in the radiance of the sun.
But they are fastened
as with seven seals

157

until Christ shall come
garbed in warrior dress,
Whose Word, like a two edged sword
shall pierce the heart,
and commence the opening of the seven seals.

And the seven sacred planets
will shine forth the light of the seven rays.
And the seven chakras shall open one by one.
Archaic remnants
sealed in the murky depths of unconsciousness
shall spill out like plagues.

A great battle shall ensue
between the seven lords who serve Christ
and the seven shadow lords
who serve selfish desire.
When the battle is fought and won,
the seven chakras
shall become as seven kings.
The kings shall be wise men
and shall be the new rulers of man's being.
The inner kingdom shall grow green again,
and rise up out of the charred ruins of destruction.

Then the seven kings
who are the seven wise men
shall kneel in homage
to the new born Christ.

And the awakened heart shall avert the apocalypse.

The Seven Perfections issued forth from the seven stars to the seven churches—from the outermost to the innermost reaches of my soul. They shone forth their truth and beauty, quality and virtue—in *seven rays* of Colour, illuminating all that was dark and unwholesome in the Spirit realms of man.

Colour was their transmittance, through which their consciousness was revealed.

And I came to the centre of being and learned the mysteries of initiation, priesthood, kingship and prophecy...

Illuminated with the grace of the heart, I entered the virgin rain forest. It was the culmination of my initiation. There, I was given the task for which only God named me.

That day was the eleventh day of the eleventh month, 1989.

John the Divine in his Apocalyptic vision said there were four beasts 'round the throne of God...*The first was a lion, and the second beast like a calf, and the third beast had a face as a man, and the fourth beast was like a flying eagle.*

These beasts are symbolic of the Fixed Cross of the heavens. The lion was Leo. The calf was Taurus. The beast with the face of a man was Aquarius. And the eagle flying was Scorpio. When sexual energy is transmuted, the symbol for Scorpio is not a scorpion, but an eagle flying. The eagle is a bird with great vision that sees from afar. Hence it symbolises the awakened third eye.

These prophecies refer to the ending of an old era. The time is now. This is the eleventh hour. Humanity is destined to mount the Fixed Cross of the Heavens. Apocalyptic events shall come to pass.

When the angel passed me the white cylindrical object of light, it signified there was to be a New Covenant with the earth. White is a synthesis of all seven rainbow colours. This is the new Rainbow Bridge linking Humanity with the heavens.

All these years later, the passage of time has brought to full maturity the significance of this event:

> It was the angel's initiation,
> mine also,
> and foretold the great collective initiation
> Humanity was destined to undergo.

The angel had achieved liberation from this planet. It was the last of its kind—of the life-chain that had guarded and stimulated the developing physical and sentient nature of humankind and maintained the balance

159

of nature. Now it was time for the children of the earth to grow up and learn the hidden *science of relationship.*

A new chain of spiritual hierarchy will stimulate the developing consciousness of humankind. This chain of hierarchy will express itself through the sign of Leo—shadow sign of Aquarius. It will stimulate and facilitate humankind's individuation process. Humanity must individuate in order to serve the Group Being and thus take one step closer to realising the destiny that is written in the stars.

This new spiritual hierarchy is not our guardian angel. We are truly all alone—poised on the brink of great spiritual opportunity or apocalyptic destruction. But as we struggle to raise our consciousness, this new chain of spiritual hierarchy will gradually be enabled to come to meet us more fully.

They are the great angels who radiate the Seven Rays of rainbow Colour throughout the universe. They are our new teachers—seven archetypal perfections, hovering over cosmic imperfection. Coming in contact with them, their perfect vibration will tune the consciousness of Humanity and raise it to the Spirit realm. Humanity will learn the language of Colour and thus for the first time gain direct *spirit knowledge.*

In the spirit of the New Age, which is the spirit of service, this new chain of hierarchy will serve only those of us who care. Only by awakening our hearts will we be able to hear their music and speak their language.

When Parsifal at last finds the Holy Grail, he must address his Chalice and ask the question, "Whom does the Grail serve?" If we listen hard enough to the quietest of all inner voices we will hear it answer—*only those who care, those pure in heart.*

And only the pure in heart shall avert the apocalypse.

Epilogue

MRITA bid me close this book with words of John the Divine taken from the *Book of Revelations:*

And I saw in the right hand of him that sat on the throne a book written within and on the backside, sealed with seven seals.

And I saw a strong angel proclaiming with a loud voice, who is worthy to open the book, neither to look thereon.

And I wept much, because no man was found worthy to open and to read the book, neither to look thereon. And one of the elders saith unto me, Weep not: behold the *Lion of the tribe of Juda*, the *Root of David*, hath prevailed to open the book, and to loose the seven seals thereof.

And I beheld, and, lo, in the midst of the throne and of the four beasts, and in the midst of the elders, stood a Lamb as it had been slain, having seven horns and seven eyes, which are the Seven Spirits of God, sent forth into all the earth.

And he came and took the book out of the right hand of him that sat upon the throne.

And when he had taken the book, the four beasts and four and twenty elders fell down before the Lamb, having every one of them harps, and golden vials full of odours, which are the prayers of saints.

And they sang a new song, saying, Thou art worthy to take the book, and to open the seals thereof: for thou wast slain and has redeemed us to God by thy blood out of every kindred, and tongue, and people, and nation; And hast made us unto our God kings and priests: and we shall reign on the earth.

161